Exploring **DINOSAURS** with Mr Hibb

Discovering evidence for creation

Michael J. Oard, Gary Bates, Tara Wolfe & Chris Turbuck

Exploring Dinosaurs with Mr Hibb: Discovering evidence for creation
by Michael J. Oard, Gary Bates, Tara Wolfe, Chris Turbuck

First printing: July 2016

ISBN 978-1-942773-22-1

Cover Design: Daniel Lovelace and Keaton Halley
Layout: Daniel Lovelace and Keaton Halley

Unless specified otherwise, Scripture quotations are from The Holy Bible, English Standard Version® (ESV®), copyright © 2001 by Crossway, a publishing ministry of Good News Publishers. Used by permission.

Published by:

Creation Book Publishers
P.O. Box 350
Powder Springs, Georgia, 30127 USA
Phone: 1-800-616-1264
www.creationbookpublishers.com

For further information on creation/evolution
and the Christian worldview, go to

CREATION.com

Exploring
DINOSAURS
with Mr Hibb

Michael J. Oard, Gary Bates,
Tara Wolfe & Chris Turbuck

Acknowledgements

A book is a team effort. We are thankful first of all to Beverly Oard, who edited an earlier manuscript. We appreciate Caleb Salisbury for coloring the diagrams and Jacob Oard for drawing one figure. We thank Dr Tas Walker and Lita Cosner of *Creation Ministries International* (CMI) for all their editorial work, and we are grateful that *Creation Book Publishers* took on the project and set up the material in a digestible manner for young people. We also appreciate the work of Daniel Lovelace and Keaton Halley for laying out the book in a timely manner.

Table of Contents

= activities for you to do!

By Michael J. Oard and Gary Bates

People, both young and old, love dinosaurs. But, probably more than any other topic, the secular worldview of dinosaurs hooks people into believing in evolution and its millions of years as a scientific fact. This causes many to doubt the Bible's early chapters and results in loss of faith for many. However, the true facts about dinosaurs tell a different story—facts we can use to show the Bible is true.

This second book in the popular Mr Hibb series is a fun way for people of all ages to look through the eyes of the inquisitive character Mr Hibb—an intelligent, imaginary grasshopper. In the previous book, *Exploring Geology with Mr Hibb*, the groundwork was laid showing how the concept of millions of years came about. It was a reinterpretation of the facts of geology through the assumption of slow processes over millions of years—uniformitarianism. This caused the shift from the biblical 'young' world with a global Flood to an old world with no catastrophes forming the geological layers. Biological evolution soon resulted from this major shift in thinking.

So, the billions of fossils found in the sedimentary record were placed, then viewed, as evidence for millions of years of slow gradual process and the evolution of life on Earth. But with a correct biblical worldview a totally different picture emerges. In this book we focus on how to interpret dinosaur fossils biblically.

We will demonstrate that dinosaurs did not live millions of years ago and the vast majority of dinosaurs perished and were buried in Noah's Flood. A correct understanding of the great Flood of Noah's time helps us solve many of the long-age time challenges presented by the secular world. We can then demonstrate how the various biblical 'kinds' of dinosaurs could have survived that great Flood by being occupants on Noah's Ark. There is incredible evidence to suggest that some dinosaurs may have lived until quite recently.

In addition, the millions of dinosaur tracks, eggs, and scavenged bonebeds found all over the world are great evidence resulting from the chaos early in the Flood when dinosaurs tried to escape rising floodwaters.

It is important for all Christians to know what the Bible really says. A well-grounded biblical worldview can help young and old alike see the world around us as it should be—that is, in the light of true biblical history.

—∞—

Chapter 1

Those Terrible Lizards

Mr Hibb is not just any insect. He is a unique, very curious grasshopper. He doesn't mean to get into trouble or find himself in dangerous situations, it just seems to happen. He is fascinated by the world around him and thankful to his Creator, God.

Mr Hibb has a new interest: dinosaurs. It started when he went on a dinosaur roller coaster at a theme park. The mechanical *T. rex* fascinated him, and frightened him a little too. It had such big teeth.

It seems just about everyone is fascinated by dinosaurs, but why? It could be because some of them were the largest land creatures that ever lived, and our imaginations can run wild thinking what it would be like if we could see them alive today. To this end, there have been lots of movies and television shows made that draw millions of people to dinosaurs every year. Museums even have models of these amazing creatures. Like many others, you might even have a dinosaur toy or two. But do the movies, models, and even science books truthfully show what dinosaurs were really like, and when they actually lived? While some aspects of these may be truthful, they are often accompanied by a lot of make-believe storytelling. We'll talk more about that later.

Dinosaurs were very different from creatures alive today. Although they look a little bit like some of the lizards that exist today, many dinosaurs were massive in size and had huge, fearsome-looking teeth. Mr Hibb looked up the name 'dinosaur'. *It is a Greek word which literally means 'fearsome or terrible lizard'.* We will tell you how they came to be called terrible lizards a bit later.

HANDS-ON ACTIVITY
Make A Play-Doh Dinosaur

Obtain play-doh and make a dinosaur shown in this book. For skin or scale impressions, you can use a cheese grater (preferably a small one) and impress into play-doh. You can also use toothpicks to provide skin texture. For horns or spikes, you can use cashews, macaroni, etc. Be creative and have fun.

What you'll need
• play-doh
• textured objects

Looking at his lizard friend, Izzy, Mr Hibb could see he looked similar, well kind of. Because we don't see dinosaurs today, we face a lot of mysteries when studying them. For example, where did they come from and what happened to them?

What is a Dinosaur?

What exactly is a dinosaur and how is it different from reptiles living today? Classifying reptiles is sometimes difficult because they may have features that overlap into other groups such as birds and even mammals. One feature of dinosaurs is that they have legs that go beneath them to support their weight—almost like the columns we see on buildings that support a structure. Reptile limbs flare out to the sides. There are many reptiles in the fossil record (the collection of fossils so far) as well as many different types that live today. From the fossil record one of the largest reptiles that ever lived was *Dimetrodon*. It was about 10 feet (3 metres) long with what looks like a sail sticking up and running along its back. Actually, the 'sail' was made up from a series of long vertebrae or backbones that protruded from its body. Some scientists think the *Dimetrodon* was more mammal-like than reptilian because certain features of its skull were similar to those of a mammal.

Dinosaur

Lizard

DEFINITION

Dinosaur   An extinct reptile-like creature with legs that extend straight below the body to support its weight.

Dimetrodon

How Do We Know Dinosaurs Actually Existed?

We know dinosaurs existed because we find their fossils buried in sedimentary rocks. Sedimentary rock is a type of rock formed when particles of minerals (like sand or mud) and other broken pieces of rock were laid down by water or wind and cemented together. Dissolved chemicals, such as silica

(silicon dioxide) are carried by water. Silica is the same mineral found in quartz and the glass used in windows. This very special water goes through the spaces (pores) in the sediment and joins the particles together like concrete to become rock.[1]

A fossil is any evidence of life preserved in a rock. It could be a creature, plant, or any object from the past. Dinosaur fossils can include bones, impressions of their skin, their eggs, or even their footprints or tracks. Many fossil bones have become rock hard because chemicals were absorbed into them from the surrounding water or mud before they rotted. (This process is called *permineralization.*) Sometimes we find dinosaur bones that have not hardened into stone.

DEFINITION

Permineralization	A process of preservation whereby the original hard parts of an animal have additional mineral material deposited in their pore spaces.

Two Types of Dinosaurs

Scientists that study fossils are called *paleontologists*. They group or split dinosaurs into two basic types, depending upon the shape of the dinosaur's hip. These types can be described as the lizard-hipped and the bird-hipped dinosaurs. The hips of bird-like dinosaurs are similar to the hips of birds because the two long bones, the ischium and pubis, that spread out from the top of the hip bend sharply toward the tail. The bird-hipped dinosaurs include those that were described as duck-billed dinosaurs. These included

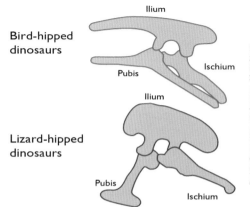

Bird-hipped dinosaurs

Lizard-hipped dinosaurs

Ilium

Pubis

Ischium

Ilium

Pubis

Ischium

Fred the Oyster, Wikimedia Commons CC BY-SA 4.0

DINOSAURS

LIZARD-HIPPED

BIRD-HIPPED

SAUROPODS
(4-FOOTED,
LONG NECK)

THEROPODS
(MEAT-EATING,
WALKED ON
HIND LEGS)

HADROSAURS
(DUCK-BILLED)

TRICERATOPS

families of dinosaurs called hadrosaurs, and Ceratopsia. The Ceratopsia included the famous three-horned dinosaur called *Triceratops*.

There are two subtypes of lizard-hipped dinosaurs and it is easy to understand the difference. The first group is the large four-footed dinosaurs with long necks and long tails. These are called sauropods and include the huge beasts called *Diplodocus* and *Brachiosaurus*. This group once included the famous *Brontosaurus*. But would you believe *Brontosaurus* was rejected as a real dinosaur in the 1970s, but many paleontologists want to bring it back? We will explain why, later.

DEFINITION

Sauropod	A group of dinosaurs that had a long neck and tail, five-toed limbs, and a small head.
Theropod	A group of often large dinosaurs that walked on their hind legs, and had large jaws and short arms.

Mr Hibb's Dinosaur Facts

Brachiosaurus
(brack-ee-uh-sore-us)

Meaning
Arm lizard

Length
100 feet (30.5 metres)

Weight
60 US tons (54 tonnes)

Distribution
Africa, North America,
and Europe

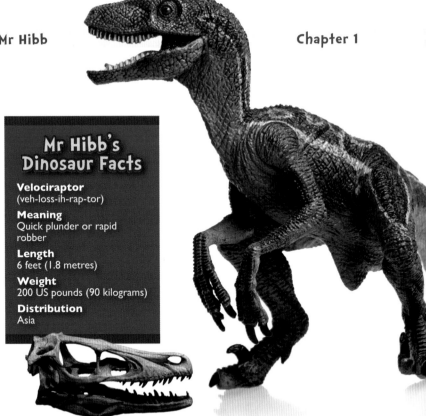

The second subtype of lizard-hipped dinosaurs are called theropods. These are dinosaurs that walked on two hind legs and generally had short arms. They varied in size from large to small (just like the sauropods). This group included probably the most famous dinosaurs of all, the ferocious looking *Tyrannosaurus rex* (*T. rex* for short) and *Velociraptor*, who was the 'nasty' star in the movie *Jurassic Park*.

Mr Hibb's Dinosaur Facts

Velociraptor
(veh-loss-ih-rap-tor)

Meaning
Quick plunder or rapid robber

Length
6 feet (1.8 metres)

Weight
200 US pounds (90 kilograms)

Distribution
Asia

Velociraptor skull

Marine and Flying Reptiles

Dinosaurs lived on land, but we also find dinosaur-like creatures that could either swim or fly.

Those that swam are called marine reptiles and many were large and fierce looking.[2] One of the most familiar groups of marine reptiles is the plesiosaurs. They had a long neck and huge flippers. The ichthyosaur is another familiar marine reptile that had large round eyes and looked a bit like today's porpoises or dolphins (which are classified as mammals) but much larger. Probably the fiercest looking of all the marine reptiles was mighty *Mosasaurus*,

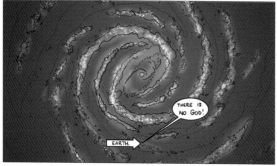

which grew up to 50 feet (15 metres) long. With fearsome-looking teeth it was often considered the *T. rex* of the deep.

There were also flying reptiles called pterosaurs that once filled the skies. These had long necks and tails and a greatly extended fourth 'finger' that spread out their canvas-like wings. They kind of looked like giant bats. The most well-known flying reptile was *Pteranodon* which had a wing span up to 30 feet (9 metres) and had a long backwards pointing skull. Scientists are still puzzled over

the reason for such a weird-shaped head. One huge pterosaur was called *Quetzalcoatlus*. It had a wing span of up to 40 feet (12 metres) and was the size of a small airplane. It was probably the largest flying creature ever. Like airplanes today it would have cast a large shadow on the ground as it flew overhead. Mr Hibb hears a small plane and because he is studying dinosaurs, instantly thinks the plane is a flying reptile.

DEFINITION

Marine reptile	Reptiles that lived or currently live in water. Some, like the *Plesiosaur*, have become extinct.
Flying reptile	Reptiles that could fly, like *Pteranodon*, which are now extinct.

Mr Hibb's Dinosaur Facts

Plesiosaur
(plee-zee-uh-sore)

Meaning
Close to lizard

Length
50 feet (15 metres)

Weight
12 US tons (10.8 tonnes)

Distribution
Worldwide

Warm or Cold-Blooded?

Reptiles are cold-blooded, unlike human beings who are warm-blooded. Reptiles need to be warmed by the sun or warm air. You may have seen lizards, for example, standing still in the sunlight. They survive best in warm climates, and that's why we often see lots of reptiles in deserts around the world. Some scientists believe that dinosaurs were cold-blooded, too. Others believe they were warm-blooded, and still others think they were neither. No one knows for sure.

Did They Live in Swamps?

You have probably seen lots of pictures of dinosaurs living in swamps. Some reptiles today, like alligators and crocodiles, live in swamps. Some dinosaurs probably lived in swamps, but many would be unsuited to that environment, particularly the bigger ones. They would probably get stuck in mud, for example. Many had bodies that were not suited for swimming, like *Triceratops* with its heavy spiked head and *Stegosaurus* with huge armour plates on its back.

Early Discoveries of Dinosaurs

Science is about observing and investigating. Just as in many areas of science, what we know about dinosaurs has changed over time. Dinosaur research is a relatively new area of science. Because people today have never viewed living dinosaurs, some scientists have put fossilized bones

Mr Hibb's Dinosaur Facts

Pteranodon
(te-ran-uh-don)

Meaning
Winged and toothless

Length
30 feet (9 metres)

Weight
132 US pounds (60 kilograms)

Distribution
Europe, North America, Asia

together in the wrong order and sometimes on the wrong creatures. This led to all sorts of crazy claims about the first dinosaurs discovered.

The First Dinosaur Tooth Found

Scientists really knew very little about the dinosaurs of the past. There are many claims and different stories about who

DEFINITION

| **Taxonomy** | The science of classifying plants and animals into different categories, and describing them. |

discovered the first dinosaur bones and when. People were probably finding bones and fossils for hundreds of years, but did not know what they were. Modern science seeks to understand our world. In the area of biology, it seeks to name and classify all living things on the earth—a study called taxonomy. Research into dinosaurs really took off in 1822 when the wife of a man named Gideon Mantell found several large fossilized teeth. Regardless of who first discovered dinosaurs, large bones were also found. The bones and teeth ended up belonging to the duck-billed dinosaur, *Iguanodon.* Mantell had difficulty convincing the scientific community of his time that he had discovered a unique creature.

Strange Imaginary Beasts

At first, scientists did not know what kind of creatures they were looking at. All they had were fossilized bones, mainly just some parts of skeletons. It's not surprising that many of the early reconstructions, in which they tried to piece the dinosaur together, looked very different

Iguanodon

from the way dinosaurs would have actually been. Mantell's *Iguanodon* was made to look like a large iguana lizard, which is what inspired its name.

About the same time as Gideon Mantell's discovery, William Buckland pieced together some fossils and called the strange beast *Megalosaurus*. Again, these

are Greek words. Mega means 'great' and saurus means 'reptile'. It was 30 feet (9 metres) long and weighed about two US tons (over 2,000 kilograms). Early reconstructions depicted it as a big lizard that walked on all four legs. Today, it is considered a meat-eating dinosaur that walked on two legs, a bit like a small *Tyrannosaurus rex*.

Sir Richard Owen Named Them in 1841

It was finally realized that these terrible lizard-like creatures once existed as a distinct group. Many more fossilized bones were unearthed and dinosaurs started

Mr Hibb's Dinosaur Facts

Megalosaurus
(meg-uh-lo-sore-us)

Meaning
Great lizard

Length
30 feet (9 metres)

Weight
2 US tons (1.8 tonnes)

Distribution
Europe

to be studied at many universities. The study of fossils is called *paleontology*. Scientists needed to give the bones a name or *classification*. Sir Richard Owen, a famous British scientist, named them dinosaurs (dinosauria) in 1841. Keep in mind that this was the very first time the name dinosaur was used. It is a modern word.

The Bone Wars

The fascination with dinosaurs really took off in the late 1800s when many new discoveries were made, especially in the United States. Two wealthy men, Othniel Marsh and Edward Cope, competed to see who could find the biggest and best dinosaurs in the states of Montana, Wyoming, and Colorado. They dug up such familiar dinosaurs as *Diplodocus*, *Apatosaurus*, *Stegosaurus*, *Triceratops*, and *Brontosaurus*. Because of the huge public interest in dinosaurs, and sadly, due

to their rivalry, Marsh and Cope also became bitter enemies. Their field workers often spied on each other's dig sites. They lied about where they were digging in an attempt to fool their rivals. Sometimes there were even fights.

This period in dinosaur discoveries is called the 'bone wars'. It is a sad reflection of what people will do to become famous, even in the area of science, and especially in the discovery and study of fossils.

What Happened to Brontosaurus?

Brontosaurus, which means 'thunder lizard', was one of the large sauropod dinosaurs discovered and named by Othniel Marsh. *Brontosaurus* went on to become one of the most famous dinosaurs of all time, but it was later thought to be a terrible mistake. Huge, nearly complete skeletons were found and mounted in museums. However, the fossilized skeleton first found by Marsh's crew was missing a head. So, they found a head at a different location and placed it on the skeleton of *Brontosaurus*. There was one problem, however. It was the wrong head! Scientists did not discover this mistake until the late 1900s, over 100 years later. Further research claimed that *Brontosaurus* was really an *Apatosaurus*. This mistake shows how a bitter rivalry and the rush to publish and become famous can cause problems with scientific claims. However, many paleontologists want to bring *Brontosaurus* back, based on a comparison of 81 skeletons that show it was different than *Apatosaurus*.[3]

Distribution All Over the Earth

Now that scientists have discovered millions of dinosaur bones, and often just fragments of bones, they are trying to unravel which animals they belonged to and how they lived. Dinosaur fossils are found on every continent, including Antarctica. They are also found in very remote places like Siberia, Greenland, northern Canada, and Alaska. Because they are found all over the earth, it poses some interesting questions when it comes to understanding these mysterious creatures.

Polar Dinosaurs

Because dinosaur fossils have been found toward the north and south poles (that is, at high or polar latitudes) where the present climate is cold and snowy, scientists have changed their thinking about dinosaurs. Instead of living only in a warm climates, as previously thought, scientists now believe dinosaurs also lived in cold climates. This presents a puzzle about how dinosaurs can possibly live at high or polar latitudes, where it is dark for up to six months and cold for about nine months. Dinosaur expert Michael Benton expresses his frustration:

> "Should we now imagine dinosaurs as thermally insulated warm-blooded animals that ploughed through snowdrifts and scraped the ice off the ground to find food?"[4]

Two other evolutionary scientists are also mystified:

> "The picture of dinosaurs that were active in a country with permafrost, and that consequently experienced winter temperatures which only a few mammals tolerate today, is

a very different one than the popular perception of all dinosaurs as denizens [occupiers] of steaming, tropical swamps."[5]

THANKS FOR THE LEMONADE DUDE!

Finding food in such frozen wastelands would be a problem for dinosaurs in polar areas, because they needed plenty of fuel to heat their large bodies. Soon we will explain how this puzzle is easily solved.

Desert Dinosaurs

Some scientists think that dinosaurs lived not only in very cold climates but also in hot deserts. This is because their fossils have been found in sandstone which is believed to have been deposited in a desert. For instance, millions of dinosaur tracks have been found in large sandstone formations in Utah in the United States. Some of these sandstones are thought to have been an ancient Sahara-type desert, but much bigger. The idea of dinosaurs living in such a desert brings up more questions than answers for scientists. Just as in polar regions, what would dinosaurs eat and drink in a desert? Maybe their ideas about the sandstone forming in an ancient desert is incorrect.

Although these beliefs about polar and desert dinosaurs create huge puzzles to secular scientists, the evidence can be easily explained when we begin with the Genesis Flood. (See chapter 5.)

Variation in Size

Dinosaurs were not always huge like the sauropods or *T. rex*. Some were as small as a chicken, like *Compsognathus*. From the fossils that have been found, many think that the average size of dinosaurs might be about the size of a deer or an elk. Some dinosaur-like creatures swam and lived in the oceans, and some ruled the air—and they lived all over the earth. They certainly are fascinating. So, let's move on and find out what happened to these marvelous creatures.

★★★

1. Oard, M.J., Wolfe, T., and Turbuck, C., *Exploring Geology with Mr Hibb: Discovering Evidence for Creation and the Biblical Flood*, Creation Book Publishers, Powder Springs, GA, US, 2012.
2. Wieland, C., *Dragons of the Deep: Ocean Monsters Past and Present,* Master Books, Green Forest, AR, US, 2005.
3. Balter, M., Bully for Brontosaurus! *Science* **348**:168, 2015.
4. Benton, M.J., Polar dinosaurs and ancient climates, *Trends in Ecology and Evolution* **6**(1):28, 1991.
5. Rich, T.H. and Vickers-Rich, P., *Dinosaurs of Darkness*, Indiana University Press, Bloomington, IN, US, p. 165, 2000.

Mr Hibb's Dinosaur Facts

Compsognathus
(komp-soo-nay-thus)

Meaning
Elegant jaw

Length
3 feet (1 metre)

Weight
8 US pounds (3.6 kilograms)

Distribution
Europe

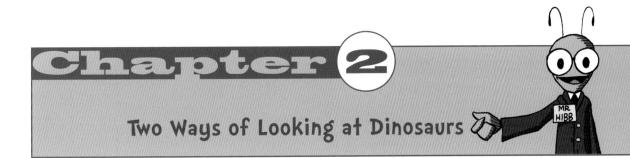

Dinosaurs are amazing creatures that lived and died in the past. Because they are not alive today it is difficult to study them. We cannot use a time machine to go back and observe how dinosaurs lived. It is very important to remember that everyone, including scientists, can only make observations in their own lifetime, that is, in the present. So, today we can only study the remains of dinosaurs by looking at their fossils and the rocks around them.

Real Science vs. Interpretation

It is important to learn the difference between what science can *actually* tell us about the things we observe, as opposed to the way people interpret or draw conclusions from those observations. When you hear the word 'science', what do you think of? Most people think of doing experiments to test things, perhaps in a laboratory. Mr Hibb especially likes

chemical experiments in the lab. Or, perhaps, you think of the inventions like the amazing rockets that can take us to the moon. This type of science can be described as 'operational science' because it deals with the way things operate. That's what we can actually *observe* in the *present*. We can also do experiments to *test* what happens and *repeat* the experiments. For example, if you wanted to see how gravity works you could drop a ball to the ground several times and you could measure the results every time.

DEFINITION

Science	It comes from Latin word *scientia*, which means knowledge. To conduct science means to organize information based upon testable explanations.
Operational science	The science that deals with the way things work in the present.

Mr Hibb's Dinosaur Facts

Tyrannosaurus rex
(tye-ran-uh-sore-us rex)

Meaning
Tyrant lizard king

Length
50 feet (15 metres)

Weight
8 US tons (7.2 tonnes)

Distribution
North America and Asia

An interpretation arises when we look at facts we can see today (in the present) and make guesses about what happened to them in the past. For example, finding a dinosaur bone in some rock strata today would be a fact. But if you hear a scientist say that it lived 65 million years ago, or that it had a really loud growl, these would be guesses or interpretations of the 'fact', as Mr Hibb has discovered. We cannot do tests on the fossil to prove when it lived and died. The interpretation you hear depends on what people believe happened in history, and people

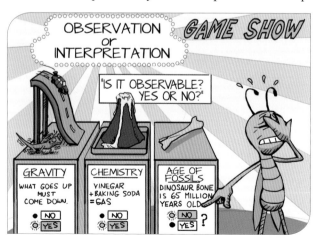

HANDS-ON ACTIVITY
Science Versus Interpretation

Science depends upon observations, but we must rely on assumptions when we try to reconstruct the past. Of the following statements, which ones are science that you observe, and which ones are interpretations?

A) The dinosaur bone was unearthed south of the city.
B) The dinosaur bone is 70 million years old.
C) Two dinosaur fossils found side by side were fighting.
D) The dinosaur skeleton was 80% complete and represents a ceratopsian.
E) Dinosaurs found in lower layers are less evolved.
F) Triceratops has three horns on his large bony head frill.
G) Dinosaurs evolved to birds.
H) There is unfossilized dinosaur material.

have different beliefs about this. It is worth remembering that rocks and fossils don't come with labels attached to tell us how old they are.

Because everyone has a belief about the past and how all life came to be on the earth, they will use their beliefs to draw conclusions about the fact. The interpretation is then claimed to be 'evidence' for their view.

Interpretations about events that occurred in the past—even what happened to the dinosaurs— depend upon the things we believe. This is also known as a worldview, and it acts like a filter or like a set of coloured glasses that causes each person to see the same facts differently.

Worldviews are ultra-important, because what you believe about where you came from will affect the way you act in the present. For example, evolutionists believe that humans

evolved from apes and that we are nothing more than evolved animals. When people believe this they may begin to wonder why they should treat other humans any better than animals. They might even act like animals. Compare this with the idea that humans were made in the image of God like the Bible says. This means that all people are valuable because we are important to our Creator God. It

DEFiNiTiON

| **Worldview** | A person's overall beliefs about the world through which they 'see' and interpret all the facts observed in the present. |

also means He created us with meaning and a purpose for us. Because He is the Creator, we are part of His creation. And, as such, we should live our lives with that idea in mind.

Also, what you believe about where you came from will affect your idea about what happens to you when you die. Many evolutionists believe that humans are just an accident, so there is no life after death. But if God is Creator, and the Bible is true, it reveals that those who trust in God will go to heaven to be with Him when they die. Can you see now why worldviews are very important?

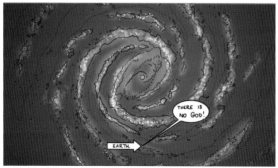

When it comes to dinosaurs, there are two main views of the past with which to interpret the fossils, tracks, and eggs of dinosaurs. These are the evolutionary or *naturalistic* worldview and the *biblical* worldview.

Using Worldviews to Interpret Our World

The Naturalistic Worldview of the Past

Naturalism (sometimes called materialism) is the belief that nature, or matter, or atoms is all there is or ever will be. This view states there is no creator and no god, no heaven, and no hell. One who believes in naturalism is often called an *atheist*. There is also a group called *agnostics*, who kind of sit on the fence by claiming that we cannot know whether God exists or not. Since atheists do not believe in God, they must believe that the universe, the Milky Way Galaxy, the solar system, the earth, and all organisms, living or extinct, came about by themselves without God. How can this happen? Naturalists believe living creatures evolved or changed from one thing to another over billions of years. But remember, how can anyone know for sure what happened in the past? The further back in time they refer to, the more their ideas become unscientific,

particularly if we do not see those things happening today.

Evolution vs. the Biblical Worldview

You may have heard of the term 'evolution'. You may have also heard some people say that evolution is a fact, but that depends what people mean when they say 'evolution'. You won't get confused by the word evolution when you understand its different meanings.

By 'evolution', most people picture the idea that simpler organisms like bacteria gradually changed into more complex ones like people over billions of years. That is one definition, but there is a second meaning that is used with living creatures. In this case, when people say evolution they mean that creatures change over time. We do see some creatures adapt or change, but this is not the same as bacteria changing into people.

Everything changes with time—even you and I will change over time.

People often look at all the varieties of dogs in the world and say that the changes between them are proof that evolution has occurred. For example, look at a Great Dane and a Poodle. Although they are very different, they are both dogs. They have different sized bones and teeth and they are different heights. But because they are both

dogs, if they breed they will only ever produce more dogs. Some of their pups might even look different from their parents. This does not prove that all life came from a simple organism, which came from chemicals, billions of years ago. That's a massive amount of change. The idea that non-living chemicals produced life is called *abiogenesis*, but real science shows that life only comes from life. This is called the *law of biogenesis*.

DEFINITION

Abiogenesis	A now-discredited belief that living organisms arise naturally from non-living matter.
The law of biogenesis	States that all life can only come from life. It is described as a law of science because it indisputably happens.

The variation that is observed in dogs does not prove that over millions of years microbes turned into math teachers! But what we actually observe (operational science) is that all living things reproduce after their own kind. To suggest that frogs turned into princes is really just like the fairy tale that you may have once heard. For

SIX DAYS OF CREATION

DAY 1
Time, space, light, and earth

DAY 2
Water and sky

DAY 3
Land and vegetation

DAY 4
Sun, moon, and stars

DAY 5
Sea and flying creatures

DAY 6
Land animals and man

instance, we can observe that horses only produce horses, apes produce other apes, and humans produce humans. This is real science and to suggest otherwise is not real science.

As we will see, dinosaurs only reproduced after their own kind. This is consistent with what the Bible says in Genesis 1. When God created the universe

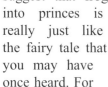

Mr Hibb's Dinosaur Facts

Stegosaurus
(steg-uh-sore-us)

Meaning
Roof reptile

Length
30 feet (9 metres)

Weight
3 US tons (2.7 tonnes)

Distribution
North America

over six days He used the phrase 'kinds' to describe the creation of living creatures. The Bible says that God made all the living creatures "after their kind" or "after his kind".

DEFINITION ①

| DNA (deoxyribo-nucleic acid) | A long, stringy molecule (a compound consisting of more than one atom) made up of a set of chemical letters that spell out the instructions for making living things and all that they do, including living, breathing, digesting, seeing, etc. |

In fact, these phrases are used 10 times in Genesis chapter 1. Modern science and Genesis have confirmed that all creatures only reproduce after their own kind, just like God said.

Amazing Design

All living creatures are made up of cells. In the nucleus of the cell there is a molecule called DNA. It is a storage system, like a hard drive on a computer, that contains a complex computer-like program or set of instructions (just like letters) that tells the cells what to build, and whether to be a dog or a frog, or to be tall or short, to have fair or dark skin, etc. DNA speaks of amazing design. You have trillions of cells in your body, and the DNA in just one of your cells could contain the same amount of information as 1,000 books of 500 pages each. The information is not in ink or in paper. The letters in the books have to be specially arranged to form words and sentences to make sense and tell a story. When you see this arrangement of letters, you instinctively know that there was an author, a greater source of information, who assembled the information. A scientist by the name of Paul Davies once said:

> "How did stupid atoms spontaneously write their own software… ? Nobody knows… … there is no known law of physics able to create information from nothing …"[1]

God literally is the 'author' of life. In the original creation, He was able to 'write' enough genetic information onto the DNA of every living creature that would allow it to reproduce, change, and survive in the future in different environments throughout the world. For example, dogs with long fur, like huskies, survive better in cold climates like Alaska, and dogs with short fur, like dingoes, might survive better in hot climates like Australia. But note again that dogs only ever change into dogs.

Those who believe in evolution thought that a lot of our DNA was 'junk', left over from previous evolutionary stages. However, scientists are now finding uses for much of that 'junk DNA'. So, if it is much more complex than we thought, then it really cannot be junk. This is just what we expect from being created.

Evolution is Unscientific

According to the theory of chemical evolution, life on earth began in some sort of chemical soup billions of years ago. The first living cell appeared as a result of unknown, natural processes, without any intelligent creator. This first cell needed to have at least hundreds of thousands of letters of information in its DNA, plus all the machinery to allow it to survive and reproduce. This all had to be present at the same time.

Then, according to the idea of biological evolution, this single celled organism supposedly evolved into multi-celled animals and then into vertebrates, over billions of years. The first vertebrate was said to be a fish, one of which somehow changed its

DNA, grew legs, developed air-breathing lungs, and crawled up onto the land as the first amphibian. Then this creature evolved into a reptile, and then certain types of reptiles turned into mammals. Then these mammals diversified and some became apes that eventually turned into people. Evolutionists also believe that dinosaurs evolved into birds by growing different types of lungs yet again, plus feathers. (See chapter 4.)

Together these two ideas are part of what is known as the General Theory of Evolution (or the GTE). Some people want to explain how *everything* came about by natural processes without God. So, they have invented even more theories to explain how the universe formed and all the stars and planets too. A more descriptive version for the evolution of life on Earth might be 'from goo to you by way of the zoo'.

DEFINITION

| **Reproduction** | The process by which new members are added to a species. |

Since real science depends upon observations, if something cannot be observed happening, then it is not science. A few evolutionary scientists have admitted that particles-to-people evolution is not ever observed. For instance, Professor David Kitts published:

"Evolution, at least in the sense that [Charles] Darwin speaks of it, cannot be detected within the lifetime of a single experimenter."[2]

However, Professor Kitts still believed in evolution even though he admitted to never seeing it happen. To turn roses into Rottweilers requires massive increases in genetic information because the differences are so great. Because they don't see these changes occurring, evolutionists, like Professor Kitts, claim that the changes may have been too small to observe. That is, it might have taken tens of thousands of really tiny steps over many millions of years, and humans do not live long enough to observe them.

If no one can observe evolution happening, then it is not a scientific fact. It is just a belief about the past based on the naturalistic worldview. Many scientists steadfastly hold to this view in spite of the lack of evidence. However, as we shall see, the arguments are not really about science. They have everything to do with whether the Creator God exists or not.

How Did Evolutionary Theory Come About?

You may have heard that Charles Darwin came up with the idea of biological evolution. But such ideas can be traced back at least 2,500 years, to the ancient Greeks, to around 700 BC (before Christ came to the earth). The Greeks probably adapted their ideas from the Babylonian, Egyptian, and Indian Hindu cultures before them. They believed in a form of *spontaneous*

OBSERVATION

Scientific interpretations can change based on new discoveries. Science is not just about 'facts'. The only area we can be sure of is operational science, where we can observe, test, and repeat things in the present.

generation, or the idea that life arose from non-living chemicals. For example, the ancients saw frogs come out of the water. Evolutionists today still believe life came from non-living chemicals millions of years ago to produce the first cell.

But the modern idea of evolution started back in the 1700s in what is called the 'Age of Enlightenment'. Scientific practices and the discovery of the natural world increased, and scholars increasingly rejected the Bible and its history of Creation, a global Flood, and the multiplication of languages at the Tower of Babel that initially caused different people groups to move out around the world. This was because they placed their own opinions and thoughts as the final authority above God's Word,

DEFINITION

| **Geology** | The study of the earth and the rocks from which it is formed. |

and attempted to explain the world using only naturalistic processes. The idea was appealing because it also meant that man did not have to listen to God. That's called sin!

But keep this in mind—science is also about discovery. Tomorrow, we might discover something we did not know about today. Therefore, it is impossible and a bit prideful to claim that we can know everything there is to know, especially about a past we were not there to see.

As time went on, more and more scholars adopted the Age of Enlightenment's views, until today naturalistic evolution is taught in our schools as fact and is accepted by most people.

The Earth Automatically Became 'Old'

Since the time when scholars decided to increasingly reject the Bible's account of creation, scientists have also invented many ideas to explain how everything came about without God. An idea called the *big bang* supposedly explains how the universe, the sun, Earth, and all the planets came into existence out of nothing billions of years ago. On the earth, they tried to explain the origin of the rocks and explain the features they observed on the surface of the earth. A Bible-believing scientist called Nicolaus Steno made great discoveries about how rocks and fossils were formed. He understood that most of the things he observed could be

Mr Hibb is not just any insect. He is a unique, very curious grasshopper. He doesn't mean to get into trouble or find himself in dangerous situations, it just seems to happen. He is fascinated by the world around him and thankful to his Creator, God.

Mr Hibb has a new interest: dinosaurs. It started when he went on a dinosaur roller coaster at a theme park. The mechanical *T. rex* fascinated him, and frightened him a little too. It had such big teeth.

It seems just about everyone is fascinated by dinosaurs, but why? It could be because some of them were the largest land creatures that ever lived, and our imaginations can run wild thinking what it would be like if we could see them alive today. To this end, there have been lots of movies and television shows made that draw millions of people to dinosaurs every year. Museums even have models of these amazing creatures. Like many others, you might even have a dinosaur toy or two. But do the movies, models, and even science books truthfully show what dinosaurs were really like, and when they actually lived? While some aspects of these may be truthful, they are often accompanied by a lot of make-believe storytelling. We'll talk more about that later.

Dinosaurs were very different from creatures alive today. Although they look a little bit like some of the lizards that exist today, many dinosaurs were massive in size and had huge, fearsome-looking teeth. Mr Hibb looked up the name 'dinosaur'. *It is a Greek word which literally means 'fearsome or terrible lizard'.* We will tell you how they came to be called terrible lizards a bit later.

HANDS-ON ACTIVITY | Make A Play-Doh Dinosaur

Obtain play-doh and make a dinosaur shown in this book. For skin or scale impressions, you can use a cheese grater (preferably a small one) and impress into play-doh. You can also use toothpicks to provide skin texture. For horns or spikes, you can use cashews, macaroni, etc. Be creative and have fun.

What you'll need
• play-doh
• textured objects

Looking at his lizard friend, Izzy, Mr Hibb could see he looked similar, well kind of. Because we don't see dinosaurs today, we face a lot of mysteries when studying them. For example, where did they come from and what happened to them?

What is a Dinosaur?

What exactly is a dinosaur and how is it different from reptiles living today? Classifying reptiles is sometimes difficult because they may have features that overlap into other groups such as birds and even mammals. One feature of dinosaurs is that they have legs that go beneath them to support their weight—almost like the columns we see on buildings that support a structure. Reptile limbs flare out to the sides. There are many reptiles in the fossil record (the collection of fossils so far) as well as many different types that live today. From the fossil record one of the largest reptiles that ever lived was *Dimetrodon*. It was about 10 feet (3 metres) long with what looks like a sail sticking up and running along its back. Actually, the 'sail' was made up from a series of long vertebrae or backbones that protruded from its body. Some scientists think the *Dimetrodon* was more mammal-like than reptilian because certain features of its skull were similar to those of a mammal.

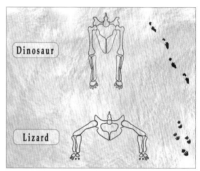

DEFINITION

Dinosaur | An extinct reptile-like creature with legs that extend straight below the body to support its weight.

Dimetrodon

explained within the framework of the biblical Flood of Noah's time. However, due to the desire of many people to explain the world without God, they came up with different ideas. One of these is called *uniformitarianism* (you-nee-form-it-airy-an-ism).

Uniformitarianism is commonly known by 'the present is the key to the past'. In other words, scientists look at processes going on today and assume that it has been going on like this unchanged for millions of years in the past. For example, we see that rainfall very slowly erodes the rocks, and that rivers carry the sediment into the sea. Uniformitarians imagine this process has been always going on like this, and it would take millions of years to erode the hills away. They imagine the rocks that we see, such as in Grand Canyon, were formed by these slow-and-gradual processes. For example, because some thin layers can be formed very slowly from water and cemented together, they reasoned that very fine rock layers were also formed by the slow process of thin

Credit: Michael Oard

sediments accumulating under watery conditions. These are called sedimentary layers. When these layers accumulate on top of one another, they form bands in the rocks called strata. Sometimes you can see these strata in the walls of canyons or mountains, such as in the Grand Canyon along the North Kaibab Trail.

The layers and the strata are 'facts'. However, no one saw them form by this slow, gradual method. Nonetheless, this became the accepted model to explain rock strata formations all over the world.

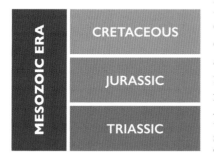

In the same way that evolutionists believe that unseen little changes occur very slowly over long periods of time to form big changes in living creatures, modern geologists believe that slow accumulation of sediments occurred over millions of years to form big layers of strata, sometimes hundreds of metres thick. (A metre is a little more than three feet.)

Naturalistic (or secular) scientists started to assign ages to the strata. The smallest grouping of the strata are called *periods*. Three of these periods were called the *Triassic*, the *Jurassic*, and the *Cretaceous*. These three periods became a subset of a larger grouping called an *era*. The *Mesozoic Era* became known as 'the great age of the dinosaurs' and allegedly covered 185 million years. We will see later that these ideas are not correct.

However, the geological facts are better explained by huge catastrophes occurring on the earth in the past. This has led to the idea of catastrophism, a view that the rocks of the earth formed rapidly during sudden and short-lived violent catastrophes. Once again, we are not able to observe that this is what actually happened in the past, but we have seen layers of strata form quickly in the present during

DEFINITION

| **Catastrophism** | The idea that the earth's geology has been shaped by sudden and short-lived violent events. |

massive earthquakes and volcanic eruptions. Noah's Flood is the best example of catastrophism, but even many naturalistic geologists who accept that catastrophes happened in the past do not accept that Noah's Flood could be a major cause. So, they have devised a scheme in which there are hundreds

Credit: Kevin Walsh, Wikimedia Commons CC BY-SA 2.0

Mr Hibb's Dinosaur Facts

Edmontosaurus
(ed-mon-tah-sore-us)

Meaning
Edmonton lizard

Length
43 feet (13 metres)

Weight
4 US tons (3.6 tonnes)

Distribution
North America

and thousands of little catastrophes, but each separated from the other by millions of years. In this way they are able to hold onto their belief in naturalism and millions of years. Millions of years are also needed to accommodate a belief in biological evolution (the slow changes that we cannot see).

Geology Led to Evolutionary Ideas

Most of the geological strata contain fossils. Fossils are the remains of creatures that once existed in the past. Because geologists assumed the rock layers to be very old, they also assumed that the fossils contained in them must have come from similarly ancient creatures that lived when the rocks were formed millions of years ago. Because they believed the rock layers form an order in history or

DEFINITION

Fossil	The remains, traces, or impressions of animals or plants that have been preserved in the earth's crust. These do not have to be turned to stone to be called a fossil.

time, they started to develop ideas that the buried creatures contained in them also formed an order in the way they evolved. According to naturalists, this history is the development of life on Earth. Their idea was that creatures changed into completely different ones over long periods of time and this became known as evolution. Charles Darwin was important in spreading the idea of evolution in the 1800s.

Dinosaurs and the Millions of Years

When dinosaur fossils were discovered in rock layers, they were given an old age based on where they were found in the strata. Creatures buried in the layers below the dinosaurs were thought to have been their evolutionary ancestors. In turn, dinosaurs became the evolutionary ancestors of creatures buried in layers above them. In short, dinosaurs were simply fit into the naturalistic idea of evolution. The story goes that dinosaurs came from or evolved from some reptile creature about 230 million years ago, and then they died out by 65 million years ago. Many believe that dinosaurs evolved into birds and that is why they are not around today. But as we shall see in chapter 6, there is great evidence that dinosaurs were still alive not long ago.

We shall also explore evidence that suggests it does not take millions of years to form rock layers. If that is the case and there is something that could have formed all the rock layers (strata) on the earth quickly, then the idea of those rocks capturing a record of animals evolving over millions of years disappears like the make believe story it really is. As we have learned, real science shows that frogs really don't turn into princes.

★★★

1. *New Scientist*, **163**(2204):27–30, 18 September 1999.
2. Kitts, D.B., Paleontology and evolutionary theory, *Evolution* **28**:466, 1974.

Chapter 3

Dinosaurs Did Not Live Millions of Years Ago

Dinosaurs were part of God's original creation. He made them along with the other land animals and the first humans on Day 6 of creation. Because dinosaurs are land animals, we know they were made on Day 6, too. They are some of the most incredible creatures that God made, but not as incredible as we—human beings—are. However, some of the dinosaurs were the biggest animals that ever walked the earth and were many times larger than humans. You could probably gain some understanding into how big they were from some of the modern names given to them by scientists. They include names like *Supersaurus* which is Latin for 'super lizard', *Titanosaurus* (titanic lizard), *Ultrasaurus* (beyond or ultra-lizard), and the incredible *Seismosaurus* (size-moe-sore-us), which literally means 'quake or earth-shaking lizard'.

All the huge dinosaurs mentioned above were *sauropods*, which have four legs, all about the same length, and usually with long necks and tails. They needed large hip and shoulder bones not only to cradle their leg muscles, but also to support the large muscles needed to hold up their neck and tail.

We should remember that in most cases paleontologists rarely find complete skeletons and sometimes find only a piece or two of vertebra (backbone). This means they have to make guesses about the missing parts. But sometimes enough of a skeleton is uncovered that they can make good guesses about

DEFINITION

Vertebra	A single piece of backbone or of the spinal column. Many call such a piece 'vertebrae' but this is the plural of vertebra. Many dinosaur vertebrae are often found as fossils.

the missing bits. The heaviest single dinosaur fossil ever found was a vertebra of *Argentinosaurus*. It was 5 x 5 feet in size (1.5 x 1.5 metres) and weighed more than 1 ton (over 1,000 kilograms). Minerals have preserved it as a fossil, so it is much heavier now than when the animal was alive.

When pieces of dinosaur fossils, like a vertebra, are found, scientists can obviously recognize it as a piece of backbone. But they do not have the rest of the pieces of the skeleton. This problem has led to believing that these fossil parts were of unique dinosaurs. It also led to the belief that there were hundreds of different dinosaur species when in many cases the fossils were just the remnants of

different-sized or different-shaped already-known dinosaurs. Try to think of how many different types of dogs you have seen. Look at the differences between a Chihuahua and a Great Dane. They have different-sized bones, even different skull shapes, as Mr Hibb noticed. But they are both dogs and members of the same family. Do you remember the 'bone wars' we described, and how they put the wrong head on the wrong dinosaur and came up with *Brontosaurus*? The frantic search to be famous and discover new dinosaurs was a major factor in this mistake—after all, everyone wants to know more about dinosaurs! It is kind of like that today.

Because we've never seen these great creatures alive today, many scientists are too quick in proclaiming their discovery of a new dinosaur. They give them fantastic names that spur our imagination regarding how big they were and what they were like. Also, do you remember that we said a scientist's beliefs are key in the way scientist interpret their discoveries? Because they believe in evolution over millions of years, they believe this gave time for possibly thousands of different dinosaurs to evolve.

As an example, let's revisit some of the supersized dinosaurs we mentioned earlier. Due to later fossil finds, we now know that *Supersaurus* is just a larger variation of the well-known *Apatosaurus,* which is

part of the *Diplodocus* family. With *Titanosaurus,* they only originally found only a few vertebrae and a couple of limb bones, and it does not appear to be much different from existing sauropods. It has been relegated to the 'trash can' as a species so one could say it has gone extinct again! *Ultrasaurus* was, unfortunately, a mixture of wrong bones again, and has been reclassified as *Supersaurus,* which we've just pointed out is really an *Apatosaurus* anyway. You can see that the study of dinosaurs is not the 'exact' science that we are often led to believe.

Oh, there's one more example. What about the *Seismosaurus?* It appears this monster dinosaur may have been as long as 170 feet (51 metres) and could have weighed over 30 US tons/60,000 pounds (over 22,000 kilograms). However, *Seismosaurus* is known to be a junior variant of the famous

Diplodocus. As you can see, when it comes to dinosaurs, there probably were not as many different kinds as you have been led to believe. We will see more on this in chapter 6.

Why do People Believe There Was a Great Age of Dinosaurs?

As mentioned, we know dinosaurs existed because we find their fossils. These are remnants of bones or impressions that have been formed in rock. Often these fossils are found in *layers* of rock called strata. This is a key to understanding why scientists view them as being millions of years old.

The Age of the Earth

The crust of the earth is covered in layered sediments that are now sedimentary rock. Sediments are dirt and rocks laid down in water or by the wind. It becomes

Credit: Keaton Halley

sedimentary rock as the particles are cemented. You can often see wide bands of sedimentary rock in mountains, canyons, and even in cuttings (where rock has been cut away from the side of hills to allow for roadways, etc.) These wide bands are the strata, but in these bands we can often find even thinner layers.

These are called lamina. They are very fine or thin layers of sediments that have been cemented together.

In the Grand Canyon, for example, you can see millions of these lamina sitting on top of one another. One of the theories (remembering that these were

Mr Hibb's Dinosaur Facts

Apatosaurus
(ah-pat-oh-sore-us)

Meaning
Deceptive lizard

Length
75 feet (23 metres)

Weight
25 US tons (22.5 tonnes)

Distribution
United States

deposited in the past and no one saw them being laid down) is that particles and sediments were slowly laid down on top of one another by water, or wind. This supposedly happens slowly today, they assume each layer may have taken up to one year to form. Then in subsequent years, more and more layers are added. So, when geologists count millions and millions of lamina in the strata, they *presume* that it took millions of years for the all the bands of strata to form. A major problem for those who want to believe that the earth is millions or even billions of years old is that we have never seen these layers form very slowly like this. Even worse, we have actually witnessed these layers forming very quickly due to catastrophic events like floods and volcanic eruptions. What happens to the millions of years if the rock layers formed quickly? Chapter 5 explains how Noah's Flood would have laid down the majority of these layers very quickly. Quite simply, the millions of years theory is really just fiction—a man-made idea. You have probably heard that scientists can do tests like radioactive dating to prove the age of rocks or fossils, but this is not entirely accurate. See later in this chapter.

The geologic column is not a record of time. It is a general order of burial of rocks and fossils due to Noah's Flood.

THE GEOLOGIC COLUMN

ERA	PERIOD	EPOCH	SUCCESSION OF LIFE
CENOZOIC recent life	QUATERNARY 0-1 Million Years Rise of Man	Recent Pleisto-cene	
	TERTIARY 62 Million Years Rise of Mammals	Pliocene Miocene Oligocene Eocene	
MESOZOIC middle life	CRETACEOUS 72 Million Years Modern seed bearing plants. Dinosaurs		
	JURASSIC 46 Million Years First birds		
	TRIASSIC 49 Million Years Cycads, first dinosaurs		
PALEOZOIC ancient life	PERMIAN 50 Million Years First reptiles		
	PENNSYLVANIAN 30 Million Years First insects	Carboniferous	
	MISSISSIPPIAN 35 Million Years Many crinoids		
	DEVONIAN 60 Million Years First seed plants, cartilage fish		
	SILURIAN 20 Million Years Earliest land animals		
	ORDOVICIAN 75 Million Years Early bony fish		
	CAMBRIAN 100 Million Years Invertebrate animals, Brachiopods, Trilobites		
	PRECAMBRIAN Very few fossils present (bacteria-algae-pollen?)		

Another piece of evidence against laminations being deposited slowly over millions of years is that tens of thousands of lamina can be bent smoothly like curves. Sometimes the dates for the lamina between the bottom and top are thought to be millions of years apart. But if this were true, one would expect that the lower layers would have hardened. The fact that the lamina did not break when bent but are smoothly folded provides evidence that they are not millions of years old, but were laid down quickly, and bent while still soft as Mr Hibb discovered.

Strata Contain Fossils

As we mentioned, an interpretation of the geologic layers led to ideas about 'deep time'. Buried throughout the strata are fossils, in fact, billions of them. Examples of nearly every kind of organism that ever lived have been found. Because there are scientists who do not want to believe that God is the Creator as described in the book of Genesis, they have tried to explain how the universe, the world, and everything in it came into existence without God. They started to believe that the organisms represented in these layers could demonstrate an evolutionary history of life on Earth over millions of years. This is how the modern theory of evolution developed. (See chapter 2 again for more on this.) They believed that the sequence or the order of burial in the fossil record could be read like a book. For instance, in the bottom layers there were 'simpler organisms', and over time they believed these evolved into more complex ones. This idea is represented in something that has become known as the geologic column. While there is a general order to the column in various places around the earth, one should not think that this

is an exact representation of what one could find if you took a slice of the earth's crust, for example.

Their belief is that life originally evolved in the seas or oceans. Then creatures grew legs and walked upon the land as amphibians. These creatures supposedly evolved into fully air-breathing creatures like reptiles, mammals, birds, and human beings. However, if the rock layers formed quickly, then the idea of deep time and millions of years evaporates. But then so does the theory of evolution based on the fossil organisms that those same rock layers contain. If, as we mentioned, Noah's Flood accounts for the formation of the majority of these layers, it means that these creatures were buried rapidly over the world about the same time, and that there was no evolution.

Everything In Six Days

According to the Bible, the only time sequence where all life first appeared on the earth was in the six days of creation described in Genesis 1. It did not take millions of years. If we accept the Bible as the real

Ankylosaurus tail club

Mr Hibb's Dinosaur Facts

Ankylosaurus
(ank-eye-low-sore-us)

Meaning
Fused or stretched lizard

Length
21 feet (6 metres)

Weight
6 US tons (5.5 tonnes)

Distribution
United States

Tail club: Domser, Wikimedia Commons CC BY-SA 3.0

history of the earth, we can actually work out when God made all the dinosaur-type creatures.

If we wanted to work out which day God made *Ankylosaurus*—a kind of armour-plated dinosaur with a bony club on the end of its tail—we just need to think logically about it. Since he was an air-breathing land animal, God made him on Day 6 along with all the other land dinosaurs.

Now, what about something like the huge flying pterosaur *Quetzalcoatlus*? He was one of the largest flying creatures that ever lived. Because he was a reptile, some might think that he was made on Day 6 because many other land animals like lizards were made on Day 6. However, *Quetzalcoatlus*

is a flying creature. Although he was reptile, he was made on Day 5. If you read your Bible, this could be a bit confusing because it might specifically say that it was birds or fowl that were created on Day 5. The Old Testament was originally written in Hebrew, a very ancient language. The Hebrew word used to describe these flying creatures looks like עוֹף which in English is pronounced 'oof'. This word was used to describe all the flying creatures, and in ancient times the word bird meant all such flying creatures. It was not until the 1700s, when a modern classification of the animals was invented, that the word bird was used to describe only those flying creatures that had feathers.

Mr Hibb's Dinosaur Facts

Quetzalcoatlus
(kwet-zal-co-at-lus)

Meaning
Feathered serpent named after a false South American god called Quetzalcoatl

Length
75 feet (23 metres)

Weight
550 US pounds (250 kilogram)

Wingspan
36 feet (11 metres)

Distribution
United States

SIX DAYS OF CREATION

DAY 1
Time, space, light, and earth

DAY 2
Water and sky

DAY 3
Land and vegetation

DAY 4
Sun, moon, and stars

DAY 5
Sea and flying creatures

DAY 6
Land animals and man

How Long Ago Was Creation?

We've said that it is not possible for scientists to do

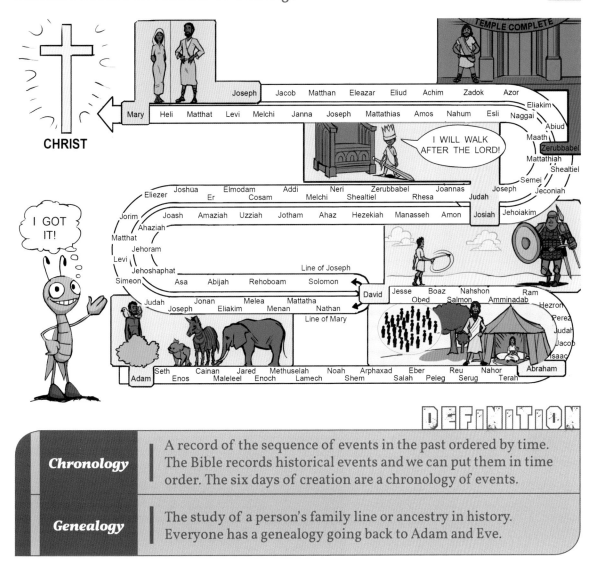

Chronology	A record of the sequence of events in the past ordered by time. The Bible records historical events and we can put them in time order. The six days of creation are a chronology of events.
Genealogy	The study of a person's family line or ancestry in history. Everyone has a genealogy going back to Adam and Eve.

tests in the present that can tell us what happened in the past. So, how can we find out how long ago God made the world and dinosaurs?

In the Bible, in both the Old and New Testaments, we can find genealogies of people arranged in chronological order, sometimes with detailed information about their ages. These show the lineage or ancestry of people in the Bible. For instance, if you read the Gospel of Luke in the New Testament, it lists Jesus' ancestry back through King Solomon, King David, Abraham, all the way back to Adam. As you can see from the illustration, at the most there are only 74 generations from Jesus to Adam through the line of Mary, Jesus' earthly mother. In addition, the Old Testament book of 1 Chronicles records similar lineages. However, in Genesis, the genealogies tell us how old the fathers were when their sons were born. It then tells us how old the sons were when they became fathers, too. We can trace all of these generations back to Adam. There are no missing generations and there is no room for millions of years in there.

A Christian theologian/historian by the name of James Ussher is famous for calculating the date of creation using the genealogies found in Scripture. He was born in 1581 and died in 1656. He was a brilliant man. Consider this: he entered university at just age 13, could speak seven different languages, and was ordained as a bishop in the Anglican Church of the United Kingdom at age

21. His main achievement was to connect the separate histories from the records of Greece, Rome, Egypt, and Israel together along with the Bible. In the process he calculated that the date of creation was around 4004 bc—that's about 6,000 years ago. It's really not difficult to calculate the date of creation from the Bible. 6,000 years is actually a very long time ago, but the main reason people think this is a very young age for creation of the earth is because wrong interpretations of geology and the millions of years have saturated our minds. Unfortunately, just about everyone has heard stories about the earth being billions of years old.

Archbishop James Ussher
(1581–1656)

People have suggested many different ways to try to fit millions of years into the Bible, so they can hold onto both. But there are big problems with all such ideas. One idea suggested is that the earth was around for millions of years before God created Adam. It is an attempt to allow enough time for all the rock layers to build up. There are big problems with this idea, so let's discuss them.

The Bible tells us that Jesus is actually God the Creator who came to earth to show us what God is like. Consider these two passages.

> "He [Jesus] is the radiance of the glory of God [the Father] and the exact imprint of his nature, and he upholds the universe by the word of his power" (Hebrews 1:3).

The above passage tells us that Jesus is *exactly* the same as God and that He controls the universe.

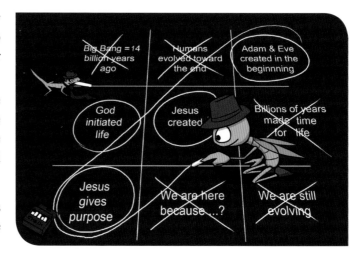

> "He [Jesus] is the image of the invisible God, the firstborn of all creation. For by him all things were created, in heaven and on earth, visible and invisible, whether thrones or dominions or rulers or authorities—all things were created through him and for him. And he is before all things, and in him all things hold together" (Colossians 1:15–17).

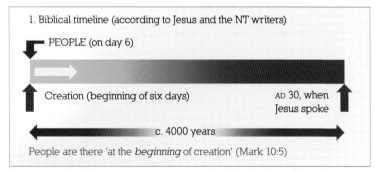

Jesus says that humans were made at the beginning of creation.

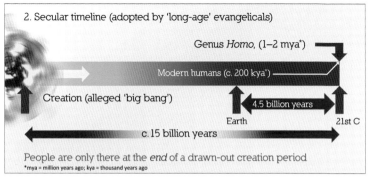

The theory of evolution puts people at the other end of creation.

This passage tells us that Jesus is the Creator. He existed before He made the universe and then He made everything in it, and He sustains it (keeps it going). These verses affirm that Jesus is God and therefore the Creator. It means we can rely upon His statement about creation. Now consider His statement in Mark 10:6–7 when He was talking about marriage. He said:

"But from the beginning of creation, 'God made them male and female. Therefore a man shall leave his father and mother and hold fast to his wife.'"

Jesus was making a point that marriage should only be between one man and one woman because that's what He made at the beginning. As the Creator and the owner of the universe, He has the right to set the rules. But also notice He said "from the beginning of creation". Creation means everything that God made—the heavens and earth. This implies that Adam and Eve, the first man and woman, were made right at the beginning, on Day 6 like the Bible says—not billions of years after the earth was made.

The General Theory of Evolution states that the universe began with a big bang about 14 billion years ago, and the earth came into existence about 4.5 billion years ago. We know from the Bible that Adam and Eve only lived a few thousand years ago. Yet, the words of the Creator Himself said they were created at the "beginning of creation". Clearly this cannot be billions or even millions of years ago. On a 14 billion year old timescale, the creation of humans only a few thousand years ago would be at the *end* of the evolutionary timeline, not at the beginning.

Evidence That Dinosaurs Did Not Live Millions of Years Ago

Biblical Evidence

There are many creatures mentioned throughout Scripture and some ask why we don't also see dinosaurs mentioned there as well. After all, they were impressive beasts! Do you recall in chapter 1 we said that the word *dinosaur* was a modern, invented word? It wasn't even in our language until after 1841. It is a modern word, just like the words computer or rocket are also modern words. You won't see those words in Scripture. We need to look for descriptions or other words that might be used to describe what we call dinosaurs today.

In the book of Job, it tells us how poor, old Job was having a very difficult time because Satan wanted to test his loyalty to God. He lost all his wealth, his children died, and he got very ill. Job was pretty depressed. After Job and his friends debated why God was doing all this to Job, God then spoke to him. In Job 40:15–19 God said:

> "Behold, Behemoth, which I made as I made you; he eats grass like an ox. Behold, his strength in his loins, and his power in the muscles of his belly. He makes his tail stiff like a cedar; the sinews of his thighs are knit together. His bones are tubes of bronze, his limbs like bars of iron. He is the first of the works of God."

Mr Hibb's Dinosaur Facts

Kronosaurus
(krow-noh-sore-us)

Meaning
Lizard of Kronos (named after a false Greek god called Cronus)

Length
33 feet (10 metres)

Weight
7–10 US tons (6–9 tonnes)

Distribution
Australia

The creature called 'Behemoth' here must be impressive because God describes it as among His 'first' works. Behemoth is described as having bones of bronze and legs of iron. Some people suggest he may have been an elephant or a hippopotamus but this does not fit. The real clue is the description of the tail which is "like a cedar". As Job lived in the Middle East, God would compare Behemoth's tail with something that Job would easily recognize. The cedars referred to are cedar trees, which are common in the area. Later in Scripture, when the wise King Solomon built the mighty temple of God, he commanded that the "cedars of Lebanon' be cut down and used (1 Kings 5:6). These cedar trees are mighty trees. Elsewhere in Scripture they are described as being "tall and lofty". This is why their wood was selected for building. We do not see any land animals today with tails like a cedar tree. The description certainly fits a sauropod dinosaur.

Also, notice that Behemoth is described as having big belly muscles. In most animals, the hip bones cradle some of the largest muscles. As a sauropod dinosaur is double hipped, it could be that God was describing its anatomy in such a way. Another description later on says:

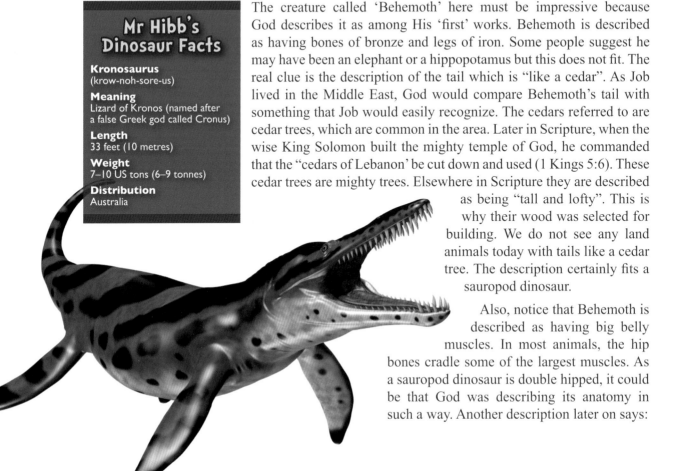

"Behold, if the river is turbulent he is not frightened; he is confident though Jordan rushes against his mouth. Can one take him by his eyes, or pierce his nose with a snare?" (Job 40:23–24).

This describes a Behemoth that can actually stand in the mighty river Jordan (the river Jordan is in the Middle East) with his mouth open against a rushing torrent. Once again, this description does not fit any land animal alive today.

Elsewhere in Scripture, there are numerous descriptions of a fearsome creature that lived in the water called *Leviathan* (see Job 3:8; 41:1, 12; Psalms 74:14; 104:26). It is possible that *Leviathan* was

a massive crocodile-like creature known as *Sarcosuchus* or even the mighty and fearsome sea creature *Kronosaurus*. It was part of the group known as pliosaurs, which are marine reptiles.

The Bible does speak about dinosaurs, although it doesn't use that word. Keep in mind that according to evolutionary theory, the last dinosaur supposedly died around 65 million years ago. But human beings were supposed to have appeared on the evolutionary scene approximately 190,000 years ago. This is over 64 million years after the last dinosaur walked the earth. Yet, the book of Job describes man and dinosaurs living together. There are more exciting records that they lived at the same time presented in chapter 6.

Scientific Evidence

The fossils of dinosaurs supposedly record how they went extinct tens of millions of years ago. Fossils are remnants of living things that have been preserved in stone. In recent years, there have been some startling discoveries of some remarkably fresh remains of dinosaurs. As far back as 1961 a petroleum geologist discovered a large, half-metre-thick bone bed in Alaska. The bones had not completely turned to stone and were mistaken for recently deposited bison bones. It took scientists over 20 years to eventually recognize them as bones from duckbill dinosaurs. Also deposited in this bed were the bones of horned dinosaurs and carnivorous dinosaurs.

In 1993, preserved red blood cells were found inside the leg bone from a *Tyrannosaurus rex*. A scientist named Mary Schweitzer helped make this discovery. She said:

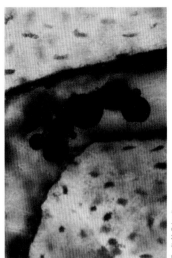

Credit: M. Schweitzer

T. rex blood cells

"It was exactly like looking at a slice of modern bone. But, of course, I couldn't believe it. I said to the lab technician: 'The bones, after all, are 65 million years old. How could blood cells survive that long?'"[1]

Did you notice how she said that the bones *were* 65 million years old? Blood degrades very quickly. It would seem almost impossible to believe that blood could remain intact for a few thousand years, let alone one million or many millions of years. But her 'pre'-belief caused her to interpret the find as millions of years old, when the evidence really suggested differently. This shows once again how people can become blinded to the truth particularly when they have only been taught one point of view.

Then in 2005, the same scientist released details of an even more astounding find. As well as more blood cells, she now found soft tissue. It was still in such good condition that Schweitzer said it was:

" … flexible and resilient and when stretched returns to its original shape."[2]

Unfossilized soft tissue samples from *T. rex* bone

Credit: M. Schweitzer

Once again this defies the idea that the last dinosaur died out 65 million years ago. It makes much more sense to believe that they lived until quite recently. (See chapter 6 for more evidence of this.)

These are not isolated examples. There have now been many cases of fresh-looking dinosaur bones being found. For example, Canadian paleontologist Philip Currie found many such bones in Alaska. When commenting on their appearance he said:

"They're as light as balsa wood and look as fresh as yesterday's dog bones."[3]

Mary Schweitzer has also discovered DNA in dinosaur bone.[4] The suggested age of the bone (80 to 85 million years old) is hundreds of times older than DNA could possibly survive under natural conditions. Schweitzer's team detected the DNA three different ways. Of course, other scientists have claimed that the bone was 'contaminated'. However, because the DNA was found in certain internal regions of the 'cells' along with the other special proteins found, contamination can be ruled out.[5] DNA in dinosaurs is powerful evidence against the millions of years of evolutionary time.

Can Scientists do Experiments to Prove the Age of Fossils?

Many believe that the millions of years have been proven by scientific tests performed on rocks and then determined for the fossils. This procedure is known as radiometric dating, and there are many different methods used depending upon the type of rock to be 'dated'. Many igneous rocks, once believed molten, contain elements that are radioactive. The radioactive atoms in the elements of these volcanic rocks continue to decay, and it is assumed that the rock keeps all the atoms trapped inside because it has solidified.

RADIOACTIVE POTASSIUM SLOWLY CHANGES INTO ARGON GAS

When the elements decay and lose their radioactive strength, they actually turn into other elements. The original element is known as the 'parent' and the element that it changes to is called the 'daughter'. For example, radioactive potassium decays into a gas called argon. Radioactive uranium turns to lead. The rate of decay is called the 'half-life', which is the time it takes for the radioactive atoms to decay by half of the original amount.

Potassium/Argon dating

half-life 1.25 billion years

Scientists can actually do experiments to measure the rate of decay, and determine what the half-life is at present rates. For example, in the case of radioactive potassium, the half-life is estimated to be 1.25 billion years based upon current measurable rates. It is often thought that because scientists know the decay rate, all they have to do is measure the amount of parent and daughter atoms in the sample to determine how old the rock is. However, there are many other things the scientist needs to know before he can make such a calculation. All of them have to do with what happened in the past. For example, in the case of potassium-argon dating, he needs to know:

- what amount of the parent element, radioactive potassium, was present in the rock when it formed

- what amount of the daughter element, argon gas, was present in the rock when it formed

- what amounts of parent and daughter elements were added or subtracted during the years

- if the radioactive decay rate has remained constant all the time.

Mr Hibb knows that radioactive potassium changes to argon gas. The assumptions can be thought of as sand in an hourglass that spreads from the top to the bottom. The fact that Izzy got in the top shows it is not a closed system.

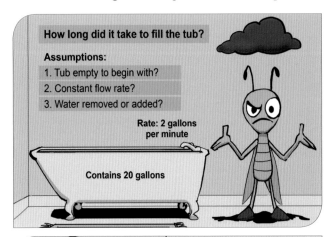

It's because of these unknowns, especially the first two, that the potassium-argon method has become popular for 'dating' rocks. The assumption is that when the magma or lava is still molten, any argon gas should escape from the liquid lava. However, it's impossible to know what the starting amount of argon was when the lava solidified. So, scientists must make an assumption on the starting amount.

They also assume that once the lava solidifies, it will trap all the argon that is produced by radioactive decay—a bit like trapping all the sand inside an hourglass. But, how does the scientist know if his assumptions are true? He doesn't. As you can see there are many unknown variables that one cannot possibly know even when doing experimental tests in the present. Here is an analogy we can use to understand this better.

Imagine that you walked into a bathroom and saw a tap running that was filling a bathtub. You want to know how long it took for the water to fill it to its present level. The first thing you would do is measure the amount of water in the bathtub. When you do, you discover that there are twenty gallons of water in it. The next thing you do is to measure the flow rate of the tap and you discover it is running at two gallons per minute. All you have to do is divide the amount of water (i.e. the radioactive potassium) by the rate the tap is running (i.e. the decay rate). Twenty gallons divided by two gallons per hour would equal ten minutes. However, you might be wrong with your answer! Why?

This is because you made assumptions.

- You presumed that the bathtub was empty when you started, but it might have been half full.

- You presumed that the tap ran at the same rate the whole time. But what if someone increased it, slowed it down, or even turned it off for a while?

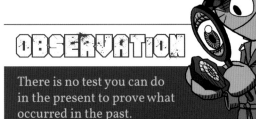

There is no test you can do in the present to prove what occurred in the past.

HANDS-ON ACTIVITY

Assumptions in Radiometric Dating

There are three main assumptions for radioactive dating as shown by the bathtub example. Obtain a plastic bottle. There are three phases to this activity.

What you'll need
- plastic bottle
- water faucet
- instrument to poke holes in bottle

A) Start filling the bottle with water, but then turn water on full force and notice that the bottle fills up faster. This demonstrates that the time to fill up the bottle depends on the rate of filling, mimicking the assumption that radioactive decay rates must remain constant throughout the past.

B) Pour out most of the water, and then refill the bottle. Notice that the time to fill the bottle cannot be known based on the present rate of filling because you had water in the bottle to start with. This mimics the assumption that you do not know how much radioactive parent and daughter were in the rock at the "beginning", usually considered the time the rock solidified from liquid rock.

C) Empty the bottle. Then start refilling the bottle very slowly, and then with a nail or other sharp instrument poke some holes into the bottom of the bottle. You cannot determine a time to fill the bottle. This mimics the assumption that the rock has to be a closed system with no parent or daughter leaking out or being added.

- Did someone add some water to the bathtub or even remove some in the past?

Mr Hibb realizes that you need to know these things in order to estimate how long it took to fill the tub.

Can you see that you were not present in the past to see these events? The only way you could definitely know that it took ten minutes was if you knew the starting conditions and watched the process the whole time. It is these types of assumptions that are made with all radiometric dating.

However, the Bible is a record of the past written by people who were there. It tells us that what the conditions of the earth were in the past. We learn from the Bible that the earth underwent a global catastrophe known as Noah's Flood. Past conditions would also have affected the past amounts of things like carbon-14, as well as other radioactive elements.

Evidence Against Millions of Years

Carbon-14 testing has provided strong evidence against the idea of a millions-of-years age for things. It has a relatively short half-life of 5,730 years compared to other radioactive elements that are used for dating methods. It can only be used to date things that contain carbon and are only thousands of years in age.

For example, according to the secular view of the geologic column, coal was supposed to have formed in peat bogs anywhere from 15 to 360 million years ago. Coal is made up predominantly of carbon. Because it is supposed to be so old, there should be no traceable amounts of any radioactive carbon-14 left. It should have all decayed away. Even if the coal were only 100,000 years old, there would be no measureable carbon-14 left. Just about every secular scientist believes in millions of years, so no one ever suspected that coal might contain significant amounts of carbon-14. A few years ago, a group of creation scientists sent samples of coal off to secular radiometric dating laboratories and every sample contained carbon-14 which should not be there if coal is millions of years old.

Edmontosaurus tailbone

The same group of scientists also had diamonds tested for carbon-14.[6] Diamonds are pure carbon and according to geologists they formed deep beneath the basement rocks of the earth, billions of years ago. Diamonds are the hardest substance we know of so they would not be contaminated by outside elements. The tests showed the diamonds contained carbon-14, which means that those billions of years theories are simply wrong.[7]

Radioactive dating cannot tell you the age of fossils, rocks, or anything that lived in the past.

Carbon-14 is now regularly found in dinosaur bones which should be impossible if they are supposed to be over 65 million years old.[8] For example, note the picture of this vertebra (actually a tailbone) from the duck-billed dinosaur *Edmontosaurus*. It was found at the Horseshoe Canyon Formation in Alberta, Canada and is supposed to be anywhere from 74–67 millions of years old. Yet, when sent to a radiometric dating lab, the tests revealed it contained carbon-14. This is scientific evidence that dinosaurs did not die out millions of years ago.

★★★

1. Schweitzer, M., quoted in Morell, V., Dino DNA: the hunt and the hype, *Science* **261**:160, 9 July 1993.

2. Scientists recover *T. rex* soft tissue: 70 million-year-old fossil yields preserved blood vessels, msnbc.msn.com/id/7285683, 24 March 2005.

3. Currie, P., quoted in Lessem, D., Explorations: Dino Thaws, *Omni* **12**(4):32 January 1990.

4. Schweitzer, M.H., Zheng, W., Cleland, T.P., and Bern, M., Molecular analyses of dinosaur osteocytes support the presence of endogenous molecules, *Bone* **52**:414–423, 2013.

5. Sarfati, J., DNA and bone cells found in a dinosaur bone, creation.com/dino-dna-bone-cells, 11 December 2012.

6. Sarfati, J., Diamonds: a creationist's best friend: Radiocarbon in diamonds: Enemy of billions of years, creation.com/diamonds, 15 August 2012.

7. Wieland, C., RATE group reveals exciting breakthroughs! creation.com/rate, 15 August 2012.

8. Thomas, B. and Nelson, V., Radiocarbon in dinosaur and other fossils, *Creation Research Society Quarterly* **51**:299–311, 2015.

Chapter 4

Why Don't We See Dinosaurs Today?

Although there have been occasional but unproven stories of dinosaur-type creatures in remote parts of the world, the fact remains that we do not see dinosaurs freely roaming around today. But, we do find millions of their remains, such as fossilized bones. We also find fossilized tracks and eggs, and as we will see, dinosaur remains are found all over the earth. (See chapter 6.) As for the very large dinosaurs, few animals would hunt them, so they had very few predators. Why are they all gone from the earth? Why are they now extinct?

Are Dinosaurs Really Extinct?

Because of reports of sightings, some people, including some scientists, believe that dinosaurs may not be extinct. They believe they could be hiding in some remote place of the world, such as the dense jungles and swamps of the Congo in Africa. An animal, which the locals called Mokele-mbembe (mo-ke-le m-bem-be) is supposed to live there in the river, but the information is uncertain. Expeditions to locate the creature have found nothing. For all practical purposes, we can assume dinosaurs are extinct.

DEFINITION

| **Extinction** | This occurs when a group of creatures or species ceases to exist. It happens when the last individual of a species dies. |

A Great Scientific Mystery

Because dinosaurs were once so abundant, their extinction baffles scientists. So much so, that there are over 100 theories about why the dinosaurs disappeared from earth.[1,2] A scientist named Glenn Jepsen declared:

> "By far the most baffling major question about dinosaurs is—What caused their extinction?"[3]

Gregory Paul sums up the puzzle quite well.

> "The history of the dinosaurs is marked by remarkable success and stability ... Far from being inherently vulnerable, the dinosaurs survived in spite of repeated changes in sea level

and climate, enormous volcanic eruptions, and great [meteorite or comet] impacts. ... Instead, it [dinosaur extinction] remains one of the most extraordinary and inexplicable [mysterious] events in Earth history."[4]

Dr. Paul doesn't believe the common notion that a meteorite impact caused dinosaur extinction. More on that later.

Extinction Ideas

Who says scientists do not have an imagination? Before scientists start their investigations, they often develop a theory, and you need an imagination to do that. They then try to test and prove their theory. Such is the case with dinosaur extinction theories. There appears to be no logical reason for the disappearance of these great creatures but scientists want explanations. However, because they were not there in the past to observe extinction events, they can only guess. They have filled in their lack of knowledge with a bewildering variety of possible explanations that range from barely believable to funny. These explanations could fill many books. Just the names of the articles about dinosaur extinction published over the past 200 years could fill one whole book.[5]

Mr Hibb's Dinosaur Facts

Deinonychus
(dye-non-ik-us)

Meaning
Terrible claw

Length
9 feet (2.7 metres)

Weight
175 US pounds (80 kilograms)

Distribution
North America

OBSERVATION

Evolutionists believe that all the animals that are alive today represent less than 1% of all the species that ever existed. This is because of their belief in the evolutionary concept of 'survival of the fittest' over millions of years.

Climate Change

It is easy to think that the dinosaurs may have died out because of climate change. Climate refers to the average weather in an area. For instance, it may be hot in the middle of North America in the summer, but cold in winter. This is the climate of that area. Also, climates can change, and so paleontologists have many ideas on how climate change could have killed off the dinosaurs. Ideas include warmer or colder temperatures, drier or wetter conditions, or more temperature extremes.

DEFINITION

| **Climate** | The average weather conditions in a region over a period of time. Statistics are gathered on such factors as temperature, humidity, wind, and atmospheric pressure. |

Then there are ideas based on the changes of air in the atmosphere. Since plants take in carbon dioxide and give off oxygen, one idea is that there was too much oxygen produced by plants. Another

idea was that there was not enough oxygen produced due to there not being enough plants on earth! Other ideas include air pollution, such as from volcanic eruptions that caused an abundance of poisonous gases, volcanic ash, or too much carbon dioxide.

Environmental Stress

There are a surprising number of suggestions that the dinosaurs died off because their environment changed. The environment refers to the surroundings in which they live. Ideas include a lot of floods, poisonous water, drainage of swamps and lakes, the presence of poisonous minerals in the soil, too much natural radiation from the sun, huge earthquakes, and sea level rises and falls.

Biological Causes

Many biological causes have been put forth. Some scientists believe that dinosaurs bred too many males, and because there were more males than females, there were not enough pairs.

Some scientists think that their eggshells became too thin and the eggs dried out. Or, that the eggshells became too thick, and the baby dinosaurs could not hatch out. Then there is the story about how the mammals increased too much and ate all the dinosaur eggs.

This is the killer-rat idea. One scientist had the strange idea that dinosaurs became so big and hungry that they ate all their own eggs. So, bye-bye dinosaurs! But the majority of dinosaurs were not really big creatures, so this explanation doesn't work.

OBSERVATION

Creationists believe that the majority of biblical kinds that God created still exist in one form or another today. Distinct kinds of land animals survived the Great Flood and many insects that were not on the Ark could have survived on floating log mats, etc. After the Flood, due to natural selection, many animals have adapted very well to post-Flood environments. See chapter 6 for more on this.

Extraterrestrial Events

Then there are a variety of extraterrestrial events (coming from outside the earth) used to explain dinosaur disappearance. These included blindness from the sun when the atmosphere allowed too many solar rays from outer space, too much cosmic radiation due to reversals in the earth's magnetic field, changes in the position of the earth poles causing rapid climate change, a huge exploding star nearby that caused the earth to be zapped with too much cosmic radiation, another moon hitting the earth, and a meteorite impact. Phew!

Ridiculous Ideas!

There are so many other ideas that we could list. For example, they became addicted to toxic plants, their brains shrunk, and they did not get enough fiber from the plants they were eating and died of constipation. Many, like those above, are just plain silly. The reason

we mention them is important because when you see so many explanations and ideas put forward, it tells you that they have no idea what really happened. They are all just guesses.

The Most Popular View—the Killer Asteroid

Scientists believe that the first dinosaurs evolved about 230 million years ago and died out suddenly at 65 million years ago. (See chapter 2 to see why they believe this.) As they supposedly roamed the

Credit: NASA, Don Davis

earth for 160 million years, why was their extinction so sudden? The most popular idea you may have heard is that a giant meteorite hit the earth and quickly wiped them out.

Starting with this theory, scientists have looked for a large crater either on the surface of the earth or buried somewhere that would be the 'smoking gun' of dinosaur extinction, as they called it. The idea became popular about 1980 when scientists discovered what they believed were tell-tale signs of an impact. They eventually found a huge crater on the sea floor off the Yucatán Peninsula in Mexico. It's called the Chicxulub Crater.

How Does an Impact Cause Extinction?

A meteorite impact would certainly kill anything close to it, but how would it kill dinosaurs that lived on the other side of the world? The best idea is that the impact blasted so much dust into the upper atmosphere that it caused a climate change by blocking out the sun, and this caused the earth to cool too much. This idea has been called 'impact winter'. It is also believed that it would have created giant tsunami waves that went around the earth.

Problems with the Impact Idea

Despite the popularity of the meteorite extinction idea, it has several serious problems. First, the buried crater on the Yucatán Peninsula is too small. The crater is now thought to be only about 120 miles (190 kilometres) across. The size of the meteorite would have been only about 6 miles (10 km) across. This is believed to be too small by many scientists to cause dinosaur extinction on a global scale. Also, some think it was not an impact crater at all, but that the crater was caused by a huge belch or burp coming from within the earth. This idea claims that gasses built up in the earth's crust eventually burst to the surface creating a giant cannon-like effect sufficient to cause climate change similar to an impact. This is pure speculation as no one has ever seen such events occur.[6]

Second, many other animals that are sensitive to cooler temperatures caused by an impact or belch did not go extinct. Crocodiles that require warm temperatures mysteriously survived. Frogs, amphibians, turtles, and lizards all survived. These survivors were also living with the dinosaurs.

Mr Hibb's Dinosaur Facts

Allosaurus
(al-uh-sore-us)

Meaning
Other lizard

Length
40 feet (12 metres)

Weight
2 US tons (1.8 tonnes)

Distribution
North America

HANDS-ON ACTIVITY
Dinosaur Extinction Theories

There are over 100 theories on the extinction of the dinosaurs. Some are given in this book. Pick one of the causes presented or make up another cause. Then draw a picture or write a story of how you think the extinction could have happened.

Third, the small dinosaurs became extinct, also. A cooler climate from a meteorite impact would cause less food, favoring the survival of small dinosaurs. This fact is contrary to the meteorite extinction idea.

A fourth major problem with the idea of a sudden drop to winter temperatures is that scientists now believe dinosaurs also lived in cold climates at polar locations, as we previously mentioned. They should have been able to survive cold temperatures from a meteorite impact.

DEFINITION

| *Paleontologist* | A scientist who studies fossils. |

Many Scientists do not Believe the Impact Idea

Although the impact idea is popular, there are many scientists who do not believe it. Paleontologists are especially critical. They claim that the dinosaurs did not all die out at one time, as expected from a meteorite hitting the earth, but gradually over a long period of time.

Dinosaurs Claimed to Not Be Extinct—Did They Evolve Into Birds?

A strange new idea has developed that dinosaurs are not extinct at all. We are not talking about the claimed sightings of Mokele-mbembe in the Congo of Africa. It is claimed that dinosaurs simply evolved to birds. Such claims are based on new discoveries from China of alleged 'feathered dinosaurs' and the long-believed 'missing link' between dinosaurs and birds called by the long name of *Archaeopteryx* (ARK-kee OP-tur-icks).[7]

Are There Really Feathered Dinosaurs?

These supposed feathered dinosaurs can be divided up into two groups. One group has bristle-like structures, which many scientists believe are simply skin structures. The second group is composed

Sinosauropteryx—some evolutionists have interpreted the bristle-like fibers along its back as 'protofeathers', but others regard them as a crest made of skin

of true feathered fossils, but, according to some scientists who study birds, the claimed dinosaurs are small and very likely just birds anyway.[8] Some extinct birds were similar to these claimed feathered dinosaurs. It is mainly a problem in how to classify extinct creatures.

Dinosaurs and birds are vastly different creatures. Dinosaurs have scales and birds have feathers, which despite their simple appearance are complex. Birds have amazing hollow bones that are very light, enabling them to fly. Their lungs are also very different. Reptiles, dinosaurs, and mammals have bellows-type lungs. Like a big paper bag, they get filled with air and are then emptied. Birds have a one way lung system. Air comes in one end and then is diffused throughout the body without breathing out. As evolution requires tiny steps of change, it is impossible to imagine how birds could have evolved from dinosaurs. The lungs have to be fully functional/operational the very first time for the creatures to breathe. So, for a dinosaur to evolve into a bird, assuming evolution, a radical change in about every characteristic of a dinosaur must have happened. There is no reason preventing some dinosaurs from being created with feathers anyway. The problem is that evolutionists claim these feathers are 'proof' that dinosaurs evolved into birds, which is not true.

Feathers under the microscope

There are many other problems with the idea that dinosaurs evolved into birds. For instance, we would expect that if evolution were true birds would have evolved from a bird-hipped dinosaur. But, would you believe, birds are claimed to have evolved from lizard-hipped dinosaurs! So, now even the hip of the dinosaur would have to be radically altered to turn it into a bird. Of course, if evolution never happened at all, then neither did the evolution of dinosaurs to birds. We do not observe evolution occurring today and we don't see the evidence in the fossil record.

Some scientists believe in feathered dinosaurs so much that they even accepted an obvious hoax. An extinct bird fossil was given a dinosaur tail and called *Archaeoraptor*, which made the pages of *National Geographic* in November, 1999. The forgery was hailed as proof of feathered dinosaurs and fooled many scientists.

A FLYING DINOSAUR?

MODEL BY STEPHEN CZERKAS

"IT'S A MISSING LINK

between terrestrial dinosaurs and birds that could actually fly."

—STEPHEN CZERKAS

Archaeoraptor—as featured in *National Geographic*, Nov. 1999, later exposed as a fraud

Missing Links?

There have always been claims of missing links in the fossil record, ever since the time of Charles Darwin. An evolutionary missing link or transitional form is supposed to be the in-between kind

Credit: Stefan Kraft, Wikimedia Commons, CC BY-SA 3.0

Platypus

of creature formed as an animal evolved from one kind into another. For example, a half-ape, half-man fossil, or half-dinosaur, half-bird kind of fossil. Many of these have just been made up because paleontologists often only find fragments of bones and not whole fossilized skeletons.

In some cases, the claimed transitional forms are probably just one of the many strange and extinct creatures in the fossil record. Even today, there are strange creatures that are difficult to classify, such as the duck-billed platypus, which has a bill like a duck, webbed feet, and a tail like a beaver, and lays eggs in the water. The fossil record is almost totally composed of distinct organisms with gaps between the various groups, which is a massive problem for evolutionists. The number of claimed transitional forms is few, whereas evolutionists need millions of these in between kinds for evolution to be true. They are called missing links because they are all still missing! The claims about missing links are often disputed by both creationists and evolutionists.

Is Archaeopteryx a Missing Link?

One organism that is believed to be a true missing link is *Archaeopteryx* found in Bavaria, Europe in 1861. It had a tail composed of extended vertebrae (backbone), teeth, and claws on its wings. But it also had 100% modern features showing even the asymmetry of flight feathers. In other words, as with all flying birds the flight feathers on the wings and tail are not the same on both sides.

However, when analyzed closely, some extinct birds also had both long tail vertebrae and teeth, while some modern birds even have claws on their wings like the hoatzin. So, it looks like *Archaeopteryx* really is a unique, extinct bird.

Public domain

Hoatzin chick with wing claws

The Biblical View—Destroyed in Noah's Flood

As you can see, scientists speculate a lot on what happened in the past. Like all the extinction ideas, when dealing with the past we should remember that a lot of guesswork is involved. Scientists will continue to be baffled as to the extinction of dinosaurs because they continue to ignore something very important. Their starting belief that the Bible is not true causes them to have a faulty interpretation of the past.

The Bible describes Noah's Flood as a global catastrophe, but it is not taken seriously by most scientists today. Our observations of dinosaur fossils and the sedimentary rock layers indicate Noah's Flood really happened, which we will explore in the next chapter.

Buried in 'Local' Floods

The appearance of many dinosaur bone beds (graveyards) sometimes show the bones all jumbled up, as if the dinosaur were torn apart and deposited in a heap. So, when scientists describe dinosaur fossils, they commonly conclude that the animals were buried in catastrophic local floods that created their fossils.

Buried Rapidly

There is a lot of evidence that dinosaurs were buried rapidly. The bones are only slightly weathered, meaning they did not lay exposed on the ground for any significant length of time before they were buried. Also, the bones show little evidence of gnawing marks or scavenging by other dinosaurs. This would be expected if the bones sat around for many days.

Huge Dinosaur Graveyards

There are also huge graveyards of dinosaurs in many places of the world, including the United States, China, and Canada. One of the largest dinosaur graveyards is northwest of Great Falls, Montana, which contains over 10,000 duck-billed dinosaurs of the same species called *Maiasaura*. The bones

Mr Hibb's Dinosaur Facts

Maiasaura
(mah-ee-ah-sore-uh)

Meaning
Good mother lizard

Length
30 feet (9 metres)

Weight
5 tons (4.5 tonnes)

Distribution
North America

are all jumbled up. It would take quite a flood with lots of water to bury these dinosaurs in such a manner. Why there is just one species will be explained in chapter 7.

It is not too difficult to add up all these 'local', catastrophic floods and conclude that the dinosaurs died out in one very big flood like the Bible describes.

Other Evidence of Rapid Burial

It is not just dinosaurs that show rapid burial in the fossil record. There are many other well-preserved fossils and numerous other graveyards containing a large number of creatures. Soft parts are even well-preserved, such as jellyfish. Some fish were buried and fossilized in the act of eating another fish or just after swallowing a fish. An ichthyosaur, an extinct marine reptile, was fossilized in the act of giving birth. A great number of creatures in the fossil record point to a global flood.

★★★

1. Oard, M.J., The extinction of the dinosaurs, *Journal of Creation* **11**(2):137–154, 1997, creation.com/dino_ex.

2. Oard, M.J., *Dinosaur Challenges and Mysteries: How the Genesis Flood Makes Sense of Dinosaur Evidence Including Tracks, Nests, Eggs, and Scavenged Bones*, Creation Book Publishers, Atlanta, GA, US, 2011.

3. Jepsen, G.L., Riddles of the terrible lizards, *American Scientist* **52**(2):231, 1964.

4. Paul, G.S., Dinosaur reproduction in the fast lane: implications of size, success, and extinction; quoted in Carpenter, K., Hirsch, K.F., and Horner, J.R. (Eds.), *Dinosaur Eggs and Babies*, Cambridge University Press, London, U.K., pp. 252–253, 1994.

5. DeCourten, F., *Dinosaurs of Utah*, The University of Utah Press, Salt Lake City, UT, US, p. 257, 1998.

6. Wieland, C., Immense impacts or big belches? *Creation* **28**(2):24–27, 2006, creation.com/immense-impacts-or-big-belches.

7. Oard, *Dinosaur Challenges*, pp. 144–155.

8. Feduccia, A., Is it a bird? Is it a dinosaur? *New Scientist* **214**(2862):28–29, 2012.

Some slow and gradual processes can be observed to lay down sediments. But Noah's Flood laid down the vast majority of sediments that hardened into sedimentary rocks and layers, also called strata. This fits in with the Bible's shorter timescale. Thus, Noah's Flood is the 'great time cruncher' for the formation of most of the world's geology. The information for Noah's Flood comes mainly from Genesis chapters 6 to 9. The Flood also buried and fossilized dinosaurs.

Credit: Jean-Christophe BENOIST, Wikimedia Commons CC BY 3.0

The Flood From Genesis

Genesis describes Noah's Flood as a huge catastrophe that covered the whole earth. Only eight people, Noah, his wife, Noah's three sons, and their wives, were saved. All the animals that lived on land and breathed air and all mankind died except for two of each of the different kinds of air-breathing land dwelling animals that God brought to the Ark.

The Ark

Noah was found to be righteous and told to build an Ark 450 feet long, 75 feet wide, and 45 feet high (137 x 23 x 14 metres). The Ark was one and a half football fields long. That is one big boat! Actually, it would be more accurate to describe it as a ship. The Ark would be especially able to float well, since its length and width compares to modern ships and barges. It seems that Noah and his sons took between 70 and 100 years to build the Ark. We have more description of the Ark in relation to dinosaurs in chapter 6.

This ship was large enough to contain a male and female of each *kind* of land animal on earth before the Flood.[1] In addition, there were seven pairs of each clean kind of animal and each kind of bird. The Bible uses the word *kinds*, which is not the same as our man-made species. (See the table of the biological classification system.) It is known that different species or even the genus classification of animals can breed together and these animals would belong to the same kind. Mr Hibb easily sees that there are different kinds that cannot interbreed, like cats and dogs. But within the kind, there is a lot of variability with different species and genera able to interbreed. Of course, all people are one kind. If the average size of the animal kind is at the genus level, there need be only about 16,000 animals on the Ark. If the average kind is at the family level, Noah only needed about 2,000 animals on the Ark! There was plenty of room on the Ark for the animals, food, and water.

Biological Classification System

God brought all the animals to Noah. Noah did not have to go and capture the animals. After all the animals were on board, God shut the door and in seven days the Flood began. The animals, or at least some of the animals, may have hibernated to make feeding them and disposing of waste easier on Noah and his family.

KINGDOM
PHYLUM
CLASS
ORDER
FAMILY
GENUS
SPECIES

Biological classification system

DEFINITION

The biblical kind	A group of animals that only produce their kind and cannot produce another kind.

The Flood Catastrophe

Genesis describes the beginning of the Flood this way:

> "In the six hundredth year of Noah's life, in the second month, on the seventeenth day of the month, on that day all the fountains of the great deep burst forth, and the windows of the heavens were opened" (Genesis 7:11).

We are not sure what exactly this verse means. The 'fountains of the great deep' suggest water coming up from the oceans or even beneath them, while the 'windows of heaven' could refer to rain coming from the sky or to the sky opening up to meteorites that impacted the earth. The net result of both mechanisms was 40 days and nights of water falling on the earth in the form of rain. The pre-Flood ocean rose and also flooded the earth. It lasted for 150 days. Genesis says that the water lifted up the Ark and continued to rise until the whole earth was completely covered by water.

> "And the waters prevailed so mightily on the earth that all the high mountains under the whole heaven were covered" (Genesis 7:19).

Since the current mountains rose up out of the floodwater (see below), the water must have covered mountains that existed either before the Flood or that uplifted early in the Flood. These mountains likely were not nearly as high as those of today. The term 'high mountains' is a matter of perspective, as Mr Hibb has learned. For instance, someone living on a flat, low plain near sea level may consider a mountain 2,000 feet (600 metres) to be high. Regardless, the Bible says that all mountains that existed on day 150 were covered with the floodwater.

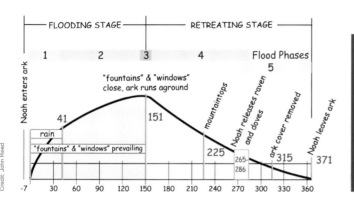

Credit: John Reed

OBSERVATION

Most of the water for the Flood came from a source beneath the ground and from the pre-Flood ocean and not from rain. Today 70% of the earth's surface is covered with water. If we lowered the current high mountains and raised the lowest valleys, there would be enough water to cover the earth to a depth of nearly 2 miles (3 kilometres).

Mr Hibb's Dinosaur Facts

Daspletosaurus
(dass-plee-tuh-sore-us)

Meaning
Frightful lizard

Length
30 feet (9 metres)

Weight
3 US tons (2.7 tonnes)

Distribution
North America
(Alberta, Canada)

The Bible then describes the Ark grounding on the 'mountains of Ararat' at day 150. After that the floodwater drained for another 221 days, making the Flood 371 days long—a little more than one year. Several more events occurred during draining of the floodwaters: Noah opened the window of the Ark, sent out a raven, and on three occasions a dove, each separated by seven days. After he discovered that the land was dry, Noah waited another two months before opening the door of the Ark so the people and animals could leave. Perhaps he was waiting for the vegetation to sprout, so the animals would have something to eat.

Log Mats Keep Some Organisms Alive

Based on the amount of coal (which is converted plant material) in sedimentary rocks, the pre-Flood forests

OBSERVATION

After the Flood, animals could have migrated to remote parts of the world on floating log mats. Shortly after Hurricanes Luis and Marilyn struck the island of Anguilla in the West Indies in 1995, local fishermen saw at least 15 green iguanas surf on to the island's eastern beaches on a natural raft up to 30 feet (9 metres) across. They had travelled over 190 miles (300 km). They have now colonized their new island home. Mr Hibb realized that such small log mats observed today would be nothing in comparison with those right after the Flood.

were lush. There were many billions of trees. The Flood would have ripped up this vegetation, and the trees not buried in sediments would end up floating on the floodwater. Thus, the log mat would be a refuge for some organisms to survive the Flood.[2] The Bible is clear that no air breathing land animals survived the Flood except for the ones on the Ark. But this does not include organisms like insects and even fish that could survive in the oceans.

The feasibility of floating log mats was dramatically shown after the eruption of Mount St Helens in 1980. The volcanic eruption downed a huge number of trees. A huge flow of rocks, dirt, and ash swept into nearby Spirit Lake causing a huge wave to sweep up the opposite slope like a mini tsunami. The water washed back into Spirit Lake carrying a million logs, with branches and leaves, into the lake. Many of these logs are still floating there to this day. Animals, insects, and other organisms rarely inhabit

I NEED TO HURRY UP!

ANGUILLA

the log mat on Spirit Lake because they can easily live on the land nearby. But, if such floating logs were the only refuge, you can be sure that the animals, insects, and other organisms would seek the log mats and attempt to live on them. It has also been shown today that some land animals can even migrate the vast distances between continents or islands on floating debris. Of course, the environment is much more sedate today than it would have been during the year-long Flood.

The Flood Was Global and Not Local

Some people, and unfortunately some religious leaders, claim that Noah's Flood was not global but local. A local flood may be a flash flood, a river flood, or possibly the bursting of an ice age lake, such as glacial Lake Missoula at the peak of the Ice Age.[3] Glacial Lake Missoula occurred in the mountains of western Montana when the edge of the ice in northern Idaho blocked a river. The lake eventually broke through the ice and caused a monstrous flood.

OBSERVATION

A million logs floating on Spirit Lake provided an example of what occurred on a much larger scale during Noah's Flood.

Genesis is written as historical narrative. This means they are recording real history just as you would read in the books of Joshua, Judges, 1 and 2 Samuel, 1 and 2 Kings, 1 and 2 Chronicles, Ezra, Nehemiah, and many other books of the Bible. Genesis 6–9 should be taken as straightforward history. There are also numerous indications from Scripture that the Flood was global. There are 30 terms in the Genesis account of the Flood that indicate a global Flood. For instance, Genesis 7:19 quoted above and many passages in the New Testament that show the authors believed it was a real global event. In another example, in 2 Peter 3:6 the Apostle Peter was referring back to the Flood when he wrote:

> "… and that by means of these the world that then existed was deluged [overflowed] with water and perished."

If the Flood was just a local event, meaning that it was small and did not cover the earth, there would be many contradictions with Scripture. After all, in the time it took Noah and his family to build it, they could have walked to

another country to escape a local flood, so, why build an Ark at all? The Ark was very large, adequate to the task of housing all the kinds of land animals, and certainly would not be needed if it was just

a local flood, as Mr Hibb realizes. Why do two of each kind of air-breathing land animal even need to be in the Ark? Why would birds need to be on the Ark if they could have just flown a few miles to a safe, dry place? If there wasn't much water, why did the Ark end up in the mountains and not down in the ocean or at the bottom of a river valley? Both man and animals were told to repopulate the earth, which would make no sense if the flood was localized. God put a rainbow in the sky as a promise to never again send such a flood again. If the flood were only local, God has broken His promise tens of thousands of times, because of all the local floods that occur. As you can see, according to the Bible, it makes no sense to presume a local flood, as Mr Hibb figured out.

And the clincher proof that the Flood was global comes from Jesus himself in Matthew 24:37–39:

"For as were the days of Noah, so will be the coming of the Son of Man. For as in those days before the flood they were eating and drinking, marrying and giving in marriage, until the day when Noah entered the ark, and they were unaware until the flood came and swept them all away, so will be the coming of the Son of Man."

Jesus believed in a real Noah, a real Ark, and that the Flood took *all people away. So should we!*

Some people try to say that "all" refers to all those in an area. They then claim these verses describe a local flood. But there is one big problem with local flood thinking and that is Jesus is using the Flood as a *comparison for his second coming. In Revelation 1:7, it says that Jesus's coming will be a worldwide event:*

> "Behold, he is coming with the clouds, and every eye will see him, even those who pierced him, and all tribes of the earth will wail on account of him."

EVIDENCE AGAINST THE LOCAL FLOOD IDEA

30 terms referring to a global Flood

The Ark saved the animals

Birds were on the Ark

The Ark ended up in the mountains

Man and animals repopulate the earth

The rainbow promise

Jesus taught a global Flood

Since Jesus is the Creator (Colossians 1:16, 17; John 1:3), He would not compare a local event with His worldwide second coming. Therefore, the Flood covered the whole earth making it global.

Why a Flood?

You may wonder why God had to send a global Flood to wipe out all mankind except those on the Ark. The Bible clearly tells us why in Genesis 6. In verse 5, it says:

> "Then the Lord saw that the wickedness of man was great on the earth, and that every intention of the thoughts of his heart was only evil continually."

They were so evil in thought and action that God would not be a God of love if He did not act. Many people would be suffering because of the many bad things occurring. He had to judge mankind and He chose a global Flood as His method.

Geology Shows a Global Flood

Some people claim that there is no evidence for a global Flood. How do they know? Were they there? Why do they say that? What evidence have they looked for?

Critics of Noah's Flood Wear Uniformitarian Glasses

As we mentioned in chapter 2, there is a remarkable human tendency of the mind to see the world through our biases. A bias can cause one to understand and see the world only one way. However, when you put a set of biblical glasses on and look around, you can see evidence for the global

Flood everywhere. Mr Hibb tries on uniformitarian glasses, which see slow processes and evolution over millions of years. He then tries creationist glasses and sees evidence for rapid deposition of layers in Noah's Flood.

Sedimentary Layers Traced Hundreds of Miles

As we discussed, sedimentary rocks can be laid down rapidly. Sedimentary rocks occur in layers and cover approximately 75% of the earth's continents. Many of these layers can run for hundreds, even thousands of miles and cover areas over a hundred thousand square miles.[4,5] Mr Hibb discovers that the layers in the southern Teton Mountains near Jackson, Wyoming (US), are nearly the same as the bottom 2/3 of the Grand Canyon, located about 500 miles (800 kilometres) away. This means they were laid down during one event. This is exactly what we expect to see

OBSERVATION

Sedimentary layers can sometimes be traced over a hundred thousand square miles. This means it took a large event to lay them, contrary to the assumption of uniformitarianism, which suggests each layer was laid down slowly over a small area.

if there had been a global Flood, whereas local floods deposit sediments only over a small area as we saw at Mount St Helens.

Where Is the Time?

Little or No Sign of Erosion Between Layers

In an earlier chapter, we discussed that secular scientists who do not accept the Bible believe that sedimentary layers were laid down slowly over millions of years. We have shown how these can be deposited quickly. This causes their ideas of old ages to disappear. Three secular geologists admitted that the sedimentary rocks of the northern and southern Teton Mountains of northwest Wyoming (US) look like they were deposited very quickly. They wrote:

> "The regularity and parallelism of the layers in well-exposed sections suggest that all these rocks were deposited in a single uninterrupted sequence."[6]

However, they still assigned ages to the rocks of over 200 million years. Since the layers show very little time for being laid down, where do these scientists put the 200 million years? Some might argue that each section or stratum may have been laid quickly and sat there for millions of years before the next deposition or sequence of layers was laid down. But there is another strong argument against this idea that demolishes the idea of millions of years.

When we look at a stack of layers, for instance, in a cliff or in the walls of the Grand Canyon, we see sandstone layers, shale layers, limestone layers, etc., one on top of the other. These layers practically always lie flat on other layers, displaying even, well defined, and sharp boundaries between them. This demonstrates that there was little or no erosion between the layers. Mr Hibb can see little, if any, evidence for erosion between layers supposedly separated by many millions of years.

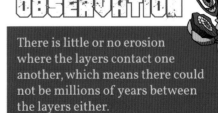

OBSERVATION

There is little or no erosion where the layers contact one another, which means there could not be millions of years between the layers either.

HANDS-ON ACTIVITY

Millions of Years of Erosion Versus Little Flood Erosion

Obtain 3 boxes of 6 oz. Jello with different colors. Make one package of Jello according to the directions on the box and pour into the bottom of a 9-by-9 inch glass pan and let set. For every package, use ½ cup of hot water mixed with ½ cup of ice water. After it sets, make "valleys" over the surface of one half of the Jello with a spoon. Make sure the valleys go to the edge of the pan. Make the second package of Jello, let it cool, and pour over the first and let set. Repeat the making of "valleys" on the same side as the first. Then make the third package of Jello and pour it over the second after it cools and let set.

What you'll need
• 3 Jello boxes of different colors, 6-oz. each
• "9x9" glass pan
• 1/2 cup measuring cup
• ice cubes
• spoon

As you examine the side of the pan, notice that in the first half, the second and third Jello layers filled in the valleys, representing erosion expected in tens to hundreds of thousands of years between and within layers of sedimentary rocks. A few million years would totally erode everything. This is the "slow erosion Jello" model. But what we find in the second half of the pan represent sedimentary rocks with no erosion (valleys) between layers. This is the "Flood Erosion Jello" model. In observing sedimentary rocks today, we actually find it fits with the "Flood Erosion Jello".

Particularly with sandstone (cemented sand), which is a relatively soft rock, much of it would have eroded away in millions of years if left to the environment. It is as if each layer was laid down rapidly one on top of the other. The little or no erosion between layers is what we expect to have occurred during Noah's Flood if they were sorted by the action of water and laid down quickly one top of one another.

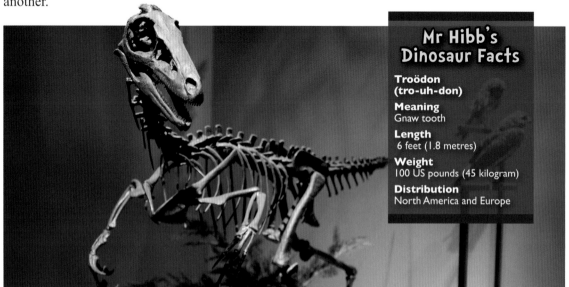

Mr Hibb's Dinosaur Facts

Troödon (tro-uh-don)

Meaning
Gnaw tooth

Length
6 feet (1.8 metres)

Weight
100 US pounds (45 kilogram)

Distribution
North America and Europe

One needs to consider the massive amount of time involved in the millions of years idea. Assuming millions of years, and using their own uniformitarian ideas of erosion, all the continents would have eroded down to sea level by now.[7]

Fossil Clams Indicate Rapid Deposition

Sedimentary rocks also contain billions of fossils, although only a very small percentage are dinosaurs. Aquatic creatures with two shells on the outside are frequently found as fossils. These are commonly called clams but they should be more accurately classified as bivalves and brachiopods.

When a clam dies, the muscles holding the shells together decay very quickly, opening the shell. Once open, even the shell can disintegrate fairly fast because it is partly made of organic matter that will rot quickly. Remarkably, these shelled animals are usually fossilized with their shells closed. The fact that we have so many *closed-shelled* clams in the fossil record indicates the sediments were deposited rapidly and the clams were buried quickly. Furthermore, since billions of closed-shelled clams are found worldwide, the deposition of sediments is evidence that it not only occurred rapidly, but that it was global, just as we expect from Noah's Flood.

Fossil clam shells, Royal Ontario Museum

Credit: Daderot, Wikimedia Commons, public domain

OBSERVATION

Most clams are fossilized with their shell closed, indicating rapid burial all over the world.

Surface Features Point to a Global Flood

Psalm 104:6–9 states how the floodwater ran off the continents:

> "You covered it with the deep as with a garment; the waters stood above the mountains. At your rebuke they fled; at the sound of your thunder they took flight. The mountains rose, the valleys sank down to the place that you appointed for them. You set a boundary that they may not pass, so that they might not again cover the earth."

These verses clearly point to the Flood since verse 6 says that God covered the land. This contrasts the description on Day 3 of creation when God 'uncovered' the land by making the dry land appear above the water. Moreover, verse 9 indicates that God set a boundary that the water may not come back to flood the earth. Verse 8 says "The mountains rose; the valleys sank down to the place that you appointed for them." So, to drain the floodwater, mountains rose and valleys sank down. At the same time the continents rose and the ocean basins sank. This also indicates massive geological activity going on during the Flood.

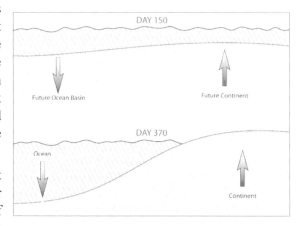

This change in elevation of the earth's crust caused the floodwater to run off the continents for 221 days, sometimes at high speeds. The runoff would have eroded the continents and mountains as they rose up out of the floodwater. We see evidence of fast and massive erosion on the continents, and the surface of the continents shows abundant evidence of this runoff by the surface features seen all over.[8,9]

One of the strongest evidences of fast Flood runoff are planation surfaces.[10] These are flat to nearly flat surfaces seen on plains, plateaus, and even mountain tops caused by the erosion of hard rock by water. We know water flattened rough land because rocks eroded and rounded by water action are found capping the hard rock. Strong water currents

OBSERVATION

Planation surfaces are observed on all continents and sometimes cover large areas, yet they are not forming today except on a very small scale.

carrying a lot of rocks must have eroded the rough land to a flat surface. Sometimes these rounded rocks come from layers hundreds of miles away and are out of place in the local surrounding geology.[11]

Planation surfaces were once much larger, but have been whittled down by further erosion. Many are still thousands of square miles in area. A few were once

A planation surface in the Bighorn Basin, Wyoming

The planation surface at top of the Grand Canyon area

over a hundred thousand square miles in area before they were further eroded. Planation surfaces are *not* forming today, except in small areas along a river bank during a flood, but they are being destroyed by present-day erosion. Mr Hibb observes a small flood eroding a walking path down to a flat surface.

Planation surfaces and rounded rocks that were transported long distances are powerful evidence for the runoff of Noah's Flood. The fact that planation surfaces are worldwide, even on the tops of some of the mountains on Antarctica that stick out above the ice, indicates the Flood was global.

A second strong evidence for the Flood on the earth's surface are water gaps. A water gap is a gorge, a canyon through mountains, a plateau, or ridge that contains a river or stream running through it. There is usually a much easier way for the river to go around the high area, but instead it appears the river 'chose' to cut right through. Since rivers do not run up and over mountains, the origin of water gaps is a major mystery of uniformitarian geology. Secular geologists have made up explanations that do not depend on a river running uphill, but these explanations rely on special conditions that

Photos: Mike Oard

Lodore Canyon, a water gap of the Green River. Uinta Mountains, Wyoming

Shoshone water gap. Rattlesnake Mountains, Wyoming

DEFINITION

Planation surface	A flat to nearly flat surface carved in hard rock by running water with a thin layer of mostly rounded rocks on top.
Water gap	A gorge that contains a river or stream and that runs through mountains.

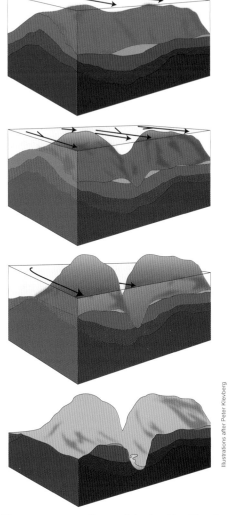

Illustrations after Peter Klevberg

How water gaps formed during the Flood

have little, if any, evidence. But the Flood can easily carve water gaps as the water was flowing against a mountain ridge or plateau. As the water was draining and/or the barrier rising, the floodwater narrows and rapidly cuts the gorge. The retreating floodwater finds a low spot on the ridge or plateau and erodes it deeply. Eventually a river or stream flows through the newly formed river valley as water runs off the hills or mountains into the valley. Mr Hibb witnesses a flood that overtopped a little hill, carving a narrow dip as a miniature water gap. There are thousands of water gaps across the earth; 1,700 exist just in the Appalachian Mountains of the eastern United States. Just like with planation surfaces, their worldwide occurrence provides strong evidence that the Flood was global.

Geological Processes Occur Rapidly

It is important to remember that the worldview of naturalism led scientists to say the earth is old primarily because of their view of geological processes and events that they see today. (See chapter 2.) Radiometric dating (see chapter 3) was only invented in the middle of the 20th century, about 200 years later than the bias toward old ages was accepted in the 1700s.

For instance, thinking of only one thin layer per year, those thick layers of sedimentary rocks were believed to be deposited over millions of years. (See chapter 3.) We have shown that the big picture of sedimentary rocks is that they were deposited rapidly as multiple layers over large areas during the Flood.[12] Surface features, such as planation surfaces and water gaps, formed quickly during Flood runoff, while uniformitarian

OBSERVATION

Thousands of water gaps are observed all over the world, and yet moderate to deep water gaps are not forming today.

Mr Hibb's Dinosaur Facts

Pachycephalosaurus
(pa-kee-sef-uh-lo-sore-us)

Meaning
Thick-headed lizard

Length
18 feet (5.5 metres)

Weight
2 US tons (1.8 tonnes)

Distribution
North America

scientists believe they formed over millions of years. These scientists have major problems coming up with any idea on the origin of planation surfaces and water gaps, even assuming millions of years.

Other time challenges to the biblical timescale can also be explained by the Flood.[13] For example, uniformitarian glasses causes most scientists to believe there were many ice ages occurring over millions of years. However, there was only one rapid Ice Age of about 700 years after the Flood.[14]

Dinosaurs Do Not Prove Millions of Years

Thus, there is no reason to believe that dinosaur fossils prove millions of years. Dinosaurs not on the Ark would have been quickly buried in Flood sediments. We do not have to be concerned about dinosaurs fossils found in cold regions today (polar dinosaurs). They could have lived at high latitude during a warm pre-Flood climate or been transported to even higher latitudes toward the poles during the Flood. There would be no such thing as desert dinosaurs because the sands were laid down in water during the Flood. The preservation of soft tissue, blood vessels, red blood cells, and now DNA is not a massive time problem as it has only been 4,500 years since the Flood. But it is a huge problem for the 65 million years since dinosaurs allegedly died out. Moreover, with the Flood we have a seeming adequate mass extinction mechanism for dinosaurs (except for those that were on the Ark, of course).

1. Woodmorappe, J., *Noah's Ark: A Feasibility Study*, Institute for Creation Research, Dallas, TX, US, 1996.

2. Oard, M.J., *The Genesis Flood and Floating Log Mats: Solving Geological Riddles*, Creation Book Publishers, Powder Springs, GA, US, 2014.

3. Oard, M.J., *The Missoula Flood Controversy and the Genesis Flood*, Creation Research Society Books, Chino Valley, AZ, US, 2004.

4. Ager, D.V., *The Nature of the Stratigraphic Record*, Macmillan, London, 1973.

5. Roth, A.A., *Origins: Linking Science and Scripture*, Review and Herald Publishing Association, Hagerstown, MD, US, pp. 218–219, 1998.

6. Love, J.D., Reed Jr, J.C., and Pierce, K.L., *Creation of the Teton Landscape: A Geological Chronicle of Jackson Hole & the Teton Range*, Greater Teton Association, Moose, WY, US, p. 42, 2007.

7. Roth, *Origins*, pp. 263–266.

8. Oard, M.J., Wolfe, T., and Turbock, C., *Exploring Geology with Mr Hibb,* Creation Book Publishers, Atlanta, GA, US, 2012.

9. Oard, M.J., *Flood by Design: Retreating Shapes the Earth's Surface*, Master Books, Green Forest, AR, US, 2008.

10. Oard, M.J., It's plain to see: flat land surfaces are strong evidence for the Genesis Flood, *Creation* **28**(2):34–37, 2006, creation.com/plain.

11. Hergenrather, J., Noah's long distance travelers: quartzite boulders speak powerfully of the global Flood, *Creation* **28**(3):30–32, 2006, creation.com/boulders.

12. Reed, J.K., and Oard, M.J., Three early arguments for deep time—part 3: the 'geognostic pile', *Journal of Creation* **26**(2):100–109, 2012, creation.com/geognostic-pile.

13. Oard, M.J. and Reed, J.K. (editors), *Rock Solid Answers: The Biblical Truth Behind 14 Geological Questions*, Master Books, Green Forest, AR, US, 2009.

14. Oard, M.J., *Frozen in Time: Woolly Mammoths, the Ice Age, and the Biblical Key to Their Secrets*, Master Books, Green Forest, AR, US, 2004.

Chapter 6

Were Dinosaurs Really on Noah's Ark?

The fact that we find millions of dinosaur fossils, including eggs and trackways, buried in sedimentary rock layers all over the earth indicates that most dinosaurs perished in the great Flood of Noah's day as described in Genesis 6–8. However, as we saw in chapter 3, God was probably describing to Job a sauropod dinosaur called *Behemoth*. Elsewhere in the book of Job we saw a reference to a marine reptile called *Leviathan.* As Job lived after the Flood, it means that some dinosaurs survived with Noah and his family and did not perish in the Flood. This is consistent with the instructions given by God to Noah in Genesis 6:19–20. He said:

> "And of every living thing of all flesh, you shall bring two of every sort into the ark to keep them alive with you. They shall be male and female. Of the birds according to their kinds, and of the animals according to their kinds, of every creeping thing of the ground, according to its kind, two of every sort shall come in to you to keep them alive."

God clearly commanded that two of every land animal (things that move along the ground) be taken aboard the Ark. He also specified that seven pairs of some creatures be taken aboard. (See Genesis 7:2–3.) Two of every land animal must have included dinosaurs and other land reptiles, which He created on Day 6 of Creation. But this creates a problem for many, because they wonder how Noah could have fit huge sauropods, like members of the *Diplodocus* family, on the Ark. The answer is really quite straightforward if we consider a few clues, as follows.

The Ark Was Massive

Unfortunately, many books you may have read picture Noah's Ark as if it is some tiny little boat—like some fairy tale from the past. But the Bible gives a pretty accurate description of its size. Mr Hibb doesn't like seeing pictures of a 'toy' ark,

Mr Hibb's Dinosaur Facts

Diplodocus
(dip-lod-oh-kuss)

Meaning
Double beamed (due to the bones in the underside of its tail)

Length
110 feet (33 metres)

Weight
18 US tons
(16 tonnes) maximum

Distribution
United States

DEFINITION

Cubit

The word *cubit* comes from the Latin word *cubitum*, which refers to the forearm. The length of a cubit was measured from the elbow to the fingertips.

because he says it causes confusion. The Bible actually tells us the size of the Ark. Genesis 6:15 says:

> "This is how you are to make it: the length of the ark 300 cubits, its breadth 50 cubits, and its height 30 cubits."

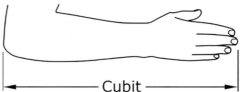

In ancient times, the size for a cubit varied between countries, but even if we used the smallest size, Noah's Ark was still a massive ship. Let's use a modest size for a cubit of 18 inches (0.46 metres or 46 centimetres). This means the Ark would have been 450 x 75 x 45 feet (140 x 23 x 13.5 m) in size.

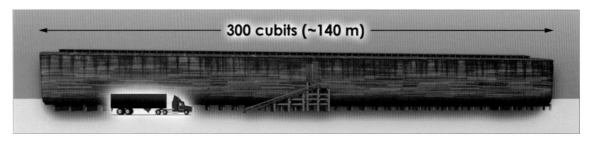

300 cubits (~140 m)

The Ark was also built with three decks. As we shall see, it was more than big enough to contain all the animals that Noah had to take on one deck. Another deck could have stored all the food, and one could have been just for Noah and his wife, their three sons and their wives.

Clue no.1: The Ark was massive and big enough for everything and everyone that needed to go aboard.

No 100-foot (30-metre) Dinosaurs Were Needed!

We've shown you that some of the dinosaurs were pretty big beasts, but even the big ones like the mighty *Diplodocus* were not always big. All dinosaurs and reptiles started off as eggs, and the largest fossilized dinosaur eggs found were about the size of a football (like a rugby ball) and were about 20 inches (50 centimetres) long. The

Bible is clear that walking animals went aboard the Ark (not eggs), so Noah could have taken young adults or teenage dinosaurs that were not fully grown yet. At this age they would have been capable of immediately reproducing after the Flood. Creationists have suggested this idea for many years,

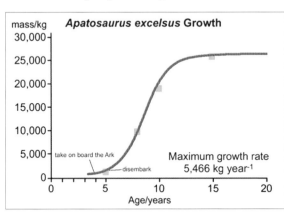

and recent fossil evidence has now confirmed this was entirely possible. Look at the graph which charts the growth spurt for *Apatosaurus*. This was based upon the growth rings found in its fossils. At about the age of 5, *Apatosaurus* was probably about the size of a large cow or bull, but then he started to grow very quickly. So quick, in fact, that he grew at the rate of about 5.5 US tons (5 tonnes) per year until he was about 13 years of age, when his growth started to slow down and level out, just like humans do.[1]

DEFINITION

Growth rings	These are the rings found in trees which record its annual growth. Often one ring is equal to one year. When the rings are wide or far apart it indicates a year of healthy or fast growth. It's the same for the dinosaur fossils mentioned above.

Clue no.2: Fully grown dinosaurs did not have to be taken on the Ark.

Not All Dinosaurs Were Large

In chapter 1, we described a very small theropod dinosaur called *Compsognathus* that is about the size of a chicken. Many theropod dinosaurs, along with lots of other types of dinosaurs, were similarly very small. Most people don't know this because of the fascination with the huge behemoths that capture our imaginations. However, the large dinosaurs were actually the exception. The smallest sauropod dinosaur seems to be *Europasaurus*. We know that this small dinosaur was fully grown because the growth rings in its fossils were very close together indicating slow adult growth.

From all the fossils we have found it looks like the average size of the dinosaur kind is that of a sheep or a large dog.

Clue no.3: Most dinosaurs were small enough to fit on the Ark.

Mr Hibb's Dinosaur Facts

Europasaurus
(you-rope-a-sore-us)

Meaning
Lizard from Europe

Length
19 feet (6 metres)

Weight
1,100 US pounds (500 kilograms)

Distribution
Europe (France, Romania)

Apatosaurus

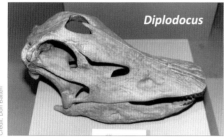

Diplodocus

Credit: Don Batten

There Were Not That Many Kinds of Dinosaurs

As we showed in chapter 3, many of the named dinosaur species were just different looking and different sized dinosaurs of the same type or biblical kind. For example, *Apatosaurus* mentioned earlier is just another variation of a *Diplodocus*. Look at the picture of the two skulls. At the top is the skull of an *Apatosaurus* and at the bottom a *Diplodocus*. Can you see how similar they are?

As mentioned, this occurs because of a faulty way of interpreting the facts, which are, in this case, two similar-looking skulls. Because of their evolutionary beliefs and the different rock layers that these creatures were found in, scientists believe they were separated by as much as 10 million years of evolution. Michael Benton, a paleontologist from the University of Bristol in the UK, explained that:

"In Victorian times, palaeontologists were keen to name new species, and in the excitement of the great 'bone wars' for example, from 1870 to 1890, they rushed into print with new names for every odd leg bone, tooth, or skull cap that came their way."[2]

Once again in recent years, dinosaur research has undergone some huge changes that only confirm that creationists were right all along. Many species of dinosaurs are being reclassified under one single group (genus). Mr Hibb understands how it is easy to get carried away and name some bones without proper analysis. These include *Nanotyrannus* which is just another *Tyrannosaurus Rex; Dracorex* and *Stygimoloch* are just young versions of *Pachycephalosaurus*. The world-famous paleontologist, Jack Horner (made famous in the *Jurassic Park* movie), has said that up to one third of all the named dinosaur species may never have really existed! Dr Hans-Dieter Sues of the National Museum of Natural History in Washington also said:

"Many dinosaurs—just like many present-day vertebrates—changed a lot in their appearance as they grew up."[3]

I'VE FOUND IT ... A SILLIORAPTOR!

UGH! IT'S A MEGALODON!

OBSERVATION

The list of the number of alleged dinosaurs that existed is shrinking all the time. It is likely that even many more dinosaurs have been wrongly classified.

For example, *Torosaurus* looks similar to the famous *Triceratops*. Although *Torosaurus* is much larger, both species have three horns. That should have been a clue that they were from the same family. It is now believed by some paleontologists that *Triceratops* is just a juvenile *Torosaurus*. However, because *Triceratops* was discovered first, the whole genus or grouping will be known as *Triceratops*. As with many creatures, their size and appearance can alter radically as they grow. Take a look at the picture at right. All of these different species are really just variants of the same original kind.

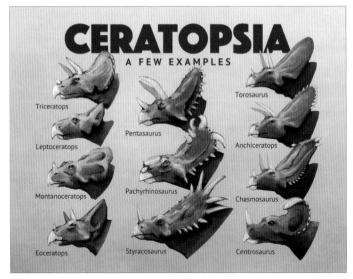

We now think there were probably only about 50 dinosaur kinds that God originally created. Let's remember that scientists often only find a few fossil bones, so there is not a lot to go on.

Clue no.4: There were not hundreds of species of dinosaurs that had to board the Ark—only about 100 dinosaurs in total (about 50 pairs).

What About Marine Reptiles?

The Bible indicates that it was only air-breathing land animals that went aboard the Ark, which would include birds and therefore the flying reptiles. It is fair to presume that many creatures, like insects and even sea creatures, possibly went extinct, but not all of them. As we have seen with local floods, and even tsunamis in recent years, huge log mats of vegetation and debris can clump together and form giant rafts—large enough for animals to survive for long periods of time. Insects and invertebrates don't really eat much. The mats could have contained enough of a food source for many larger creatures to survive.

Of course, creatures that live in the seas would have been much more likely to survive the Great Flood of Noah's time, although many of these were also buried alive and became fossilized.

OBSERVATION

Not every type of living creature on the earth was aboard the Ark, only air-breathing land animals. This means that many marine creatures and even insects may have become extinct.

Evidence of Post-Flood Dinosaurs

In chapter 3, we talked about the finds of fresh looking (unfossilized) bones and soft tissue, which is evidence that dinosaurs did not live millions of years ago. But

HANDS-ON ACTIVITY

Can Scientists Draw Dinosaurs?

Many museums have sculptures of dinosaurs. Artists try to draw or paint what the bones of a dinosaur looked like. Pretend that a paleontologist found 50% of the bones of *Dragonosaurus*. Draw what you think *Dragonosaurus* would look like? Do you think people after the Flood would be able to draw dinosaurs, such as the 800-year old bas relief found in Cambodia (see next page), without seeing them?

What you'll need

- Items for drawing or painting, such as: pencils, pens, paints and paintbrushes, crayons, etc.

there is another type of evidence that demonstrates dinosaurs lived recently—humans lived alongside living dinosaurs. This is not a problem for biblical creationists—after all, the Bible indicates that man and all the land animals were created alongside each other on Day 6 of Creation. But according to evolutionists, dinosaurs went extinct 65 million years ago, and modern humans (*Homo sapiens*) did not evolve until possibly 200,000 years ago. This means they would have been separated by 64.8 million years. Humans and dinosaurs living together is impossible for evolution, yet, you might recall how God described the mighty *behemoth* to Job, chapter 40. (See chapter 3 of this book.) Although there are some people who want to ignore the Bible, it would be hard for them to ignore the following evidence.

National flag of Wales

Humans Saw Living Dinosaurs

All around the world people have drawn pictures and told stories of dinosaur-like creatures. It is difficult to draw a creation that one has not seen, as Mr Hibb knows. We have many strange drawings of dinosaur-like creatures. Of course, they didn't call them dinosaurs. If you recall, in chapter 1, we mentioned that the word dinosaur was not invented until 1841. But the word 'dragon' seems to have been the most common word used to describe these creatures. Unfortunately, many think that dragons are mythological creatures, but this is not so. People saw them and described them. For instance, the national flag of Wales has an image of a dragon-like creature with horns on its head.

This looks a little similar to a *Triceratops,* if we keep in mind that legends can grow and be distorted over a period of time when people are trying to depict an event from the past.

Then there is the story of a brave knight named St George who fought a dragon that terrified local townspeople. St George was adopted as the patron saint of England for his deeds. Although we cannot be sure about all of these professed saints, many of them were real historical persons. All over Europe many churches and cathedrals have depictions of St George killing a creature like the pictures to the right.

Around 900 AD, an Irish author records an encounter with a beast saying it had thick legs and strong claws with a head shaped a little like a horse's. But the real clue as to what it was is in the description of it having 'iron nails' on its tail that pointed backward. This description only befits a *Stegosaurus.*[4]

In the jungles of Cambodia in South East Asia, lies a massive temple complex known as Angkor Wat. It was built by the king Suryavarmen II who lived from AD 1113–1150. It is one of the most impressive temples in the world and remained unkempt for many years until its modern rediscovery in the mid-1800s. It now attracts tens of thousands of tourists each year. On the stone walls and columns of the temple are carvings of creatures that we can easily recognize, such as monkeys, boars, and even people. But one carving has received an incredible amount of attention as it is clearly a carving of a *Stegosaurus.* The temple is 800 years old, yet they obviously knew enough about this creature to carve it accurately. *Stegosaurus* is such a unique-looking creature that it is hard to believe it was carved by chance. Clearly, they were not depicting something that died out tens of millions of years before them.

In Carlisle Cathedral, in the north of England, lies the tomb of an English Bishop by the name of Richard Bell. He died in AD 1496. Around the outside of his tomb are brass inlays or strips that are used to decorate his tomb. Similar to our previous example, the brass strips have decorative engravings of animals that are real because we can easily recognize them. See the pictures that clearly show an eel, fish,

Carvings from a temple at Angkor Wat in Cambodia

dog (with a collar!), and a bird. But take a look at the last two creatures.

These appear to be sauropod dinosaurs with long necks and long tails. They look like they are engaged in battle perhaps over a mate or territory. The one on the left has a little more detail. Notice the spikes or barbs on the end of the tail. This helps to identify it probably as a *Shunosaurus*.

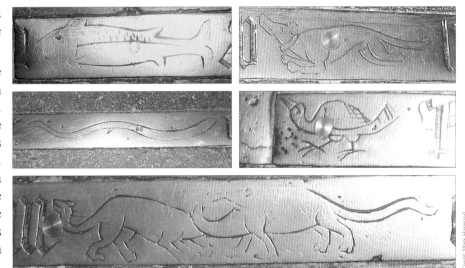

Credit: Mark Harwood

Engravings from the tomb of Bishop Bell, Carlisle Cathedral, UK

All Over the World

As we mentioned in chapter 1, dinosaurs were distributed all over the world, and similarly we see these depictions of dinosaurs/dragons in many countries. This suggests that the dinosaurs Noah took on the Ark survived and reproduced quite well and spread out over the earth. Here are more examples.

DEFINITION

| **Amphibian** | A vertebrate animal that hatches its larvae in water. It can breathe on land but can also live in water. Frogs, newts, and salamanders are amphibians. |

Mr Hibb's Dinosaur Facts

Shunosaurus
(shu-no-sore-us)

Meaning
Lizard from Shu (ancient name for Sichuan in China)

Length
31 feet (9.5 metres)

Weight
2.9 US tons (3 tonnes)

Distribution
China

China

The Chinese people have depicted dragons for centuries. The Hongshan culture carved lots of ornaments depicting dragons. Look at the jade pendant pictured to the right. It looks like a young *Protoceratops* with its distinctive head flange.

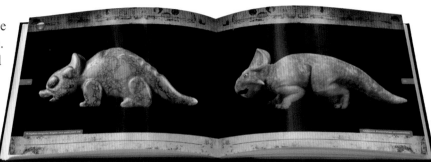

France

Chateau do Chambord in the Loire Valley of France was built as a dwelling for King Francois I who lived from AD 1515 until AD 1547 (around 470 years ago). The castle contains many statues and images on

the walls and pillars. But inside is a tapestry—actually an amazing piece of artwork. In one small section, there is what appears to be a theropod dinosaur with a lot of detail woven in. It looks a lot like the medium-sized hadrosaur known as a *Maiasaura.* Note the flat beak-shaped mouth, the position of the ear and nose holes, and the correct number of toes on its front legs. But most interesting is the depiction of scales, which have only recently been confirmed with recent fossil finds.

Middle East

Look at the creatures depicted on this ancient Mesopotamian cylinder seal. They are obviously sauropod dinosaurs with extremely long necks. These look very much like the unmistakable *Tanystropheus.*[5]

The age of the seal is around 3300 BC. Mesopotamia was an ancient country that comprised parts of modern day Iraq, Syria, Iran, and Turkey. Mr Hibb concludes that dinosaurs/dragons are found all over the world.

Post-Flood Dinosaur Populations

If dinosaur sightings after the Flood were so prolific, this begs the question of how did they reproduce so quickly and why were there so many different species stemming from around 100 individuals (50 pairs) that were on the Ark?

CHINA · CAMBODIA · ENGLAND · FRANCE · MIDDLE EAST

THEY'RE EVERYWHERE!

Earlier in this chapter and in chapter 5, we mentioned that the Bible uses the term 'kinds' to describe distinct groupings of animals, i.e. a horse kind and a dog kind and so on. Think about all the different types of dogs that you know of today. There is tremendous variation in the dog kind. Remember in chapter 3 how we compared tiny Chihuahuas to the massive Great Danes. But because all of these dogs are alive today, we understand they come from the same family group, and they can all interbreed. But just imagine if we'd never seen living Great Danes or Chihuahuas and only had their bones

OBSERVATION

All the way through recorded history, different cultures all over the world have depicted dinosaur-like creatures that supposedly went extinct millions of years before human beings allegedly evolved.

Credit: Wikipek, Wikimedia Commons CC BY-SA 3.0

Mr Hibb's Dinosaur Facts

Tanystropheus
(tan-iss-tro-fee-us)

Meaning
Greek for 'long vertebra' or long-necked one

Length
20 feet (6 metres) Its neck was as long as its body and tail combined

Weight
300 US pounds (136 kilo**grams**)

Distribution
Europe (Switzerland)

or fossils to go on. It is likely that they may have been classified as distinct separate species, or even separate genera. Earlier in this chapter, we explained how this happened with many of the alleged dinosaur species, and that many were just variations of a few original kinds of dinosaurs.

What is a Species?

No one is ever quite sure how to define what a species is anyway. What we should recognize is that species is a modern man-made word that can be used to define creatures that are sometimes merely variations of original created kinds. For example, when an organism's body structures look a lot different than the parent population it came from, or in some cases, when it can no longer interbreed with the parent population, some scientists might classify it as a new species. This is not the same as a biblical kind.

Changes in Living Things

When these original kinds of creatures change and scientists call them species, it should be remembered that they only change into variations of an original created kind. This can happen through a process of selection. This can occur in nature or it can be done purposefully, i.e. dog breeders can keep selecting increasingly small offspring to breed with one another until they produce very small dogs. In the same way, the environment can kill off dogs that don't have traits to help them survive. An example of this would be dogs with very short fur trying to survive in Alaska, US. Long fur on dogs would be a survival advantage. Those born with long hair survive, reproduce, and pass their characteristics onto their offspring. As the long furred population increases and the ones with short fur die out, eventually the only surviving dog population would be those with long fur. This is called natural selection. However, evolutionists believe natural selection to be the mechanism that can turn frogs into people over millions of years. But this is not the case. Natural selection can only 'select' from existing information that the creature possesses. Let's explain this further.

OBSERVATION

Animals can only vary or change within the existing kind that God created. Dogs and frogs can only change into dogs and frogs, and dinosaurs only changed into other variations of their original kinds also. This is not evolution.

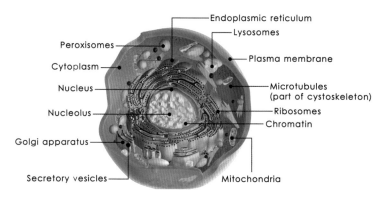

Labels: Peroxisomes, Cytoplasm, Nucleus, Nucleolus, Golgi apparatus, Secretory vesicles, Endoplasmic reticulum, Lysosomes, Plasma membrane, Microtubules (part of cystoskeleton), Ribosomes, Chromatin, Mitochondria

All living things are comprised of billions of cells. Our cells are like miniature cities that help our bodies convert, produce, and store energy and help repair our bodies. In the nucleus (the centre) of every cell is a molecule that acts like a storage system called DNA. DNA is short for deoxyribonucleic acid and contains the information for building living things.

Just imagine a hard drive on a computer or a library full of books that stores information. The DNA is so tiny that we need microscopes to see it, yet it is much more efficient at storing information than the very best computers that we can make. For example, imagine if we took the head of a dressmaker's pin and filled it with DNA. Now we take out the code or the letters of information stored in a pin head's worth of DNA and type it out into books. The pile of books would actually reach from the earth to the moon a staggering 240 times! When God created the original kinds of creatures, He loaded their DNA with so much information that enables the organism to survive and adapt when the environment changes. The world changed very rapidly at the Fall in the Garden of Eden and also after the great Flood of Noah's time.

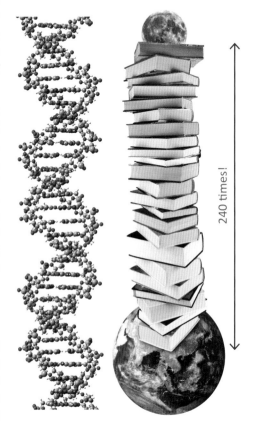

The DNA in the kinds of creatures that got off the Ark had a lot of information in their DNA so that they could produce offspring with lots of variation. For example, some dinosaurs would have been born shorter or smaller, or taller and larger. Perhaps some had slightly longer necks that helped them eat food sources in higher trees. So, as animals, including dinosaurs, migrated across the world after the Flood, they became suited to specific environments that benefitted their little differences from one another. This was all part of God's planning when he created all living things.

What Really Happened to the Dinosaurs?

In chapter 4, we discussed many of the ideas that scientists have to explain the extinction of the dinosaurs. All of them came from their beliefs in evolution and that the earth is billions of years old. Many millions of dinosaurs were killed in the Great Flood, which was around 4,500 years ago, and were fossilized in the rock layers laid down by the Flood. But in this chapter, we have seen that they seemed to be alive and well just a few hundred years ago. So, why don't we see them alive today? The answer is that we don't really know why we don't see them anymore. (See chapter 4 for more on extinction theories.) We can only guess. However, today, we do see creatures going extinct all the time—sadly, even as we speak. Mr Hibb is surprised at all the animals that have recently gone extinct. Many creatures are killed for food or simply hunted as a prize, even to the point of extinction. Man's greed has led to the close extinction of some animals, like elephants and rhinos that are hunted for their ivory tusks and horns, tigers hunted for their skins. Even some of the magnificent whales were almost hunted out of existence for their oil and meat. It is not too hard to imagine that dinosaurs were similarly hunted as a prize for food. A large dinosaur would supply enough meat for weeks or even months. We also have to remember, that the world is a relatively small place now due to our ability to travel the globe in a short time. This has enabled man to explore and catalogue most of the organisms on this planet. This helps us recognize when a species is in danger of becoming extinct. But hundreds of years ago mankind did not have this ability. Simply, if a large slow bumbling sauropod came your way—he was food!

★★★

1. Erickson, G., Makovicky, P., Currie, P., Norell, M., Yerby, S., and Brochu, C., Gigantism and comparative life-history parameters of tyrannosaurid dinosaurs, *Nature* **430**(7001):772–775, 2004.

2. Amos, J., Will the real dinosaurs stand up? *BBC News*, news.bbc.co.uk 16 August 2012.

3. Handwerk, B., A third of dinosaur species never existed? *National Geographic News*, news.nationalgeographic.com 9 October 2009.

4. Taylor, P.S., *The Great Dinosaur Mystery and the Bible*, Chariot Victor Publishing, Colorado Springs, CO, US, p. 43, 1989.

5. Moortgat, A., *The Art of Ancient Mesopotamia*, Phaidon, London, UK,1969, Plate A1.

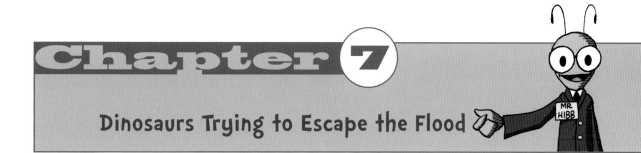

Millions of dinosaur tracks have been discovered in sedimentary rocks all over the world. Millions of eggs were also found. A dozen or more eggs are sometimes found together as if a mother dinosaur laid them in a nest. These are called egg clutches. In the dinosaur graveyards, teeth marks on bones and the broken teeth of carnivorous dinosaurs have been discovered. This means the bonebeds have been scavenged by live carnivorous dinosaurs.

Evolutionists have naturally interpreted tracks, eggs, and scavenged bonebeds within their belief system, assuming they represent normal animal behavior some one hundred million years ago. On the other hand, the Bible makes it clear that all dinosaurs living at the time, except those on the Ark, perished in Noah's Flood. At first glance, it seems difficult to explain all these dinosaur features

Dinosaur footprint

Broken dinosaur tooth

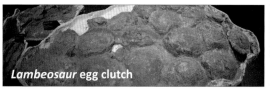

Lambeosaur egg clutch

Apatosaurus bone with teeth marks

Footprint: Greg Willis, Wikimedia Commons CC BY-SA 2.0; Tooth: Paxson Woelber, Wikimedia Commons CC BY-SA 2.0; Egg clutch: Mike Oard, Apatasaurus bone: Matt Wedel. Wikimedia Commons CC BY-SA 4.0

as formed during the Flood. A closer inspection of the details, however, demonstrates that the Flood is a more reasonable explanation.[1]

Surprising Facts on Tracks

Dinosaur tracks are a recent discovery. When examined in detail, several surprising facts emerge. The Bible tells us to examine everything carefully when presented with seemingly contradictory information. The Bible says in 1 Thessalonians 5:21: "But test everything; hold fast what is good." We are to believe God's Word, the Bible, and then check the facts.

Straight Trackways

Some trackways have dozens of tracks, so, you can follow the tracks and see the direction the dinosaur was heading. They also can tell us something about why the tracks were made. Trackways

DEFINITION 1

| **Trackway** | Two or more tracks of the same creature or dinosaur. |

Straight dinosaur trackway

Animal tracks in snow

Dinosaur tracks on a flat bedding plane

of dinosaurs are almost always straight or close to being straight. Tracks made by animals today are rarely straight unless they want to get somewhere fast, such as escaping from danger. For instance, it is well-known that deer or elk tracks found in the snow curve and zigzag all around while the animals look for food or just move from one location to another. But, if animals are spooked, then the tracks run in a generally straight direction, when there are no obstacles to dodge. Could straight dinosaur tracks mean they were escaping rising Flood water?

OBSERVATION

In nature animal tracks rarely run in straight lines as animals investigate their surroundings and forage for food—unless they are scared and need to escape danger in a hurry.

DEFINITION

| **Bedding plane** | The contact surface between two sedimentary layers or stratum. |

On One Bedding Plane

If dinosaurs were alive today, we would see them walking on dirt and climbing up and down hills. That is what we actually see animals doing. But when we examine dinosaur tracks, they are always on the surface of a flat bedding plane. Why wouldn't the tracks be found within the layers or traveling from one layer to another? Most likely it is because there was only a flat sedimentary layer to walk on at the time. Furthermore, the tracks must have been buried quickly by the next layer in order to be preserved.

Tracks of Likely Poor Swimmers Rare

Like many other animals, most dinosaurs could probably swim. Scientists can often match the track with the type of dinosaur. It has come as a surprise that the tracks of dinosaurs who were poor swimmers are rare. The likely poor swimmers include the stegosaurs, with their tall plates and spiked tail; ceratopsians (like *Triceratops*) with their thick, heavy head plate and spikes, and the ankylosaurs, with their bulky body with tails of either a heavy club or spikes, as Mr Hibb discovered. Tracks of sauropods, theropods, and duck-billed dinosaurs are common. These are the ones with powerful hind legs that would make them good swimmers. It is as if the poor swimmers drowned in a watery catastrophe, while the good swimmers escaped for awhile to make tracks on freshly laid sediments.

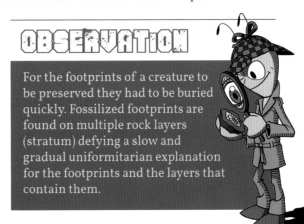

OBSERVATION

For the footprints of a creature to be preserved they had to be buried quickly. Fossilized footprints are found on multiple rock layers (stratum) defying a slow and gradual uniformitarian explanation for the footprints and the layers that contain them.

Mr Hibb's Dinosaur Facts

Parasaurolophus
(par-ah-sawr-ol-uh-fus)

Meaning
Similar crested lizard

Length
33 feet (10 metres)

Weight
4 US tons (3.6 tonnes)

Distribution
North America

HANDS-ON ACTIVITY

How Are Dinosaur Tracks Preserved?

There are billions of dinosaur tracks on flat bedding planes in the sedimentary rocks. Make tracks in mud or wet sand and then sprinkle them with water. How long do your tracks remain distinct? Why couldn't dinosaur tracks form during the first 40 days of the Flood? About how long after the making of dinosaur tracks, do you think they needed to be covered by sediment to be preserved? Was the water carrying the sediment moving slow or fast, and why?

What you'll need
- mud or wet sand
- items for making tracks—plastic dinosaur toys, plastic animals, or your own feet!
- container of water

Lack of Baby and Young Juvenile Tracks

There are other strange things concerning dinosaur tracks. The tracks of babies and juveniles are rare. When tracks of animals are seen today, around half of them are from young ones. Again, it looks like the tracks were not made in their natural environment. Similar to the rarity of the tracks of animals that were poor swimmers, babies and young dinosaurs would also be poor swimmers. It is likely they must have been swept away early by some catastrophe, leaving only the older ones to make the tracks.

Surprising Egg Facts

Just as with tracks, there are a number of surprising features observed about fossilized dinosaur eggs that reinforce the idea that the eggs were laid under unusual circumstances.

Alligator nest

Eggs Rarely Laid in Nests

Many animals make nests in which to lay their eggs, including reptiles such as crocodiles. We would expect that dinosaur eggs would often be found in nests dug into the ground to protect the eggs, but nest structures are exceedingly rare.[2]

Eggs Laid on Flat Bedding Planes with No Vegetation

Like dinosaur tracks, eggs are almost always found on flat bedding planes of sediments that have since hardened into sedimentary rocks. One would have expected that if dinosaurs did not dig nests, they would have covered their eggs with vegetation to protect the eggs and keep them warm and moist. However, little or no evidence of vegetation is ever found with the dinosaur eggs. This is indeed strange because the eggs needed to be buried rapidly to be preserved and fossilized. Any accompanying vegetation would have also been buried rapidly and fossilized.

OBSERVATION

We find millions of fossilized dinosaur eggs, billions of dinosaur tracks, and even dinosaur bodies. There are multiple lines of evidence to suggest their rapid burial in a global, watery catastrophe.

Egg Shells Porous

Under a microscope you can see that dinosaur eggs have many tiny holes in the shell. This allows oxygen from the air outside to reach the baby dinosaur inside the egg allowing it to breathe. One study found that dinosaur eggs are 8 to 16 times more porous than bird eggs.[3] This means that dinosaur eggs, laid out in the open air would dry out quickly and the baby dinosaur inside would quickly die. The way these fossilized eggs are found indicates that it was not the normal way a dinosaur would lay its eggs. Something else was going on that forced the creature to lay its eggs in such a strange fashion.

Eggs Laid In a Hurry Trying to Avoid a Watery Catastrophe

The evidence indicates that the eggs were laid in a hurry with no time to dig a nest or cover the eggs with vegetation. It seems like pregnant dinosaurs were trying to escape some catastrophe and quickly dumped their eggs wherever they could. Also, it was a watery catastrophe because water with sediments covered the eggs to preserve and fossilize them. It was a worldwide catastrophe because we see this same type of evidence all over the world.

Surprising Facts on Bonebeds

Even dinosaur bonebeds show surprising facts that indicate something unusual was happening. We have already mentioned that some dinosaur graveyards are huge and it would take a large catastrophe to bury them. But many bonebeds were scavenged,

indicating that the bones laid out in the open for a while. The dinosaur fossils are only slightly weathered and the amount of scavenging is minor. So, the graveyards did not lie around long; they must have been buried fairly quickly. But there are other unusual features with bonebeds that point away from a natural environment.

DEFINITION

| **Bonebeds** | Bonebeds are naturally occurring graveyards that contain multiple creatures. |

Sometimes the Same Type of Dinosaur

In a local flood, a volcanic catastrophe, or some other type of disaster that we read about in the newspapers, a variety of animals die. But in dinosaur graveyards, we often find mainly one type of dinosaur, which is most unusual. For instance, a graveyard of at least 1,000 small theropod dinosaurs, called *Coelophysis*, was discovered at Ghost Ranch, New Mexico, US, in 1889. The skeletons were intertwined and all the same type. The large dinosaur bonebed west of Great Falls, Montana, contains more than 10,000 duck-billed dinosaurs of the same type. What would cause such a unique accumulation? Such a mass burial would suggest some rapid catastrophic event.

Mr Hibb's Dinosaur Facts

Coelophysis
(see-lo-fise-iss)

Meaning
Hollow form

Length
9 feet (2.7 metres)

Weight
100 US pounds
(45.5 kilograms)

Distribution
North America

Mystery of the Lack of Young Dinosaurs

Catastrophes that bury animals today bury old, young, and healthy alike. We would expect a lot of young dinosaurs in dinosaur graveyards. For many it is a mystery why there are hardly any baby or young juvenile skeletons from the dinosaur graveyards found all over the earth. However, as we explain the mechanisms of the Great Flood below we might see why there were so few juvenile dinosaurs buried. Read on.

Dead Dinosaur Pose

When whole or nearly-whole dinosaurs are discovered, they often lie in a strange posture with their heads and tails bent over their backs. This has been called the dead dinosaur pose. Such a posture may have been caused by asphyxiation or

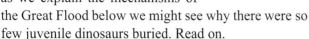

It is not only dinosaurs that appear in the dead dinosaur pose. Many creatures found in the fossil record have been affected by a similar, apparently watery, fate.

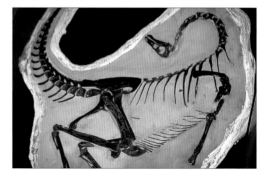

Asphyxiation	To die or lose consciousness due to having one's breathing impaired or restricted by an outside object or agency.

suffocation, like when an animal drowns or inhales volcanic ash or mud.[4] But recently, scientists discovered that dead chickens will take on this same pose if they are immersed in water. Chickens have a stretchy ligament along their spines that tries to contract after death, but the ligament cannot overcome the weight of the heavy body unless the animal is floating. So, perhaps dinosaurs had a

Mr Hibb's Dinosaur Facts

Iguanodon
(ig-won-oh-don)

Meaning
Iguana tooth

Length
33 feet (10.1 metres)

Weight
5 US tons (4.56 tonnes)

Distribution
North America, Asia, and Europe

similar ligament to help hold their heads and tails up high, and the dead dinosaur pose indicates they were floating in water just before burial.[5,6] Either explanation fits well with a global Flood.

Briefly Exposed Flood Sediments

How can the tracks, eggs, and scavenged bonebeds be explained within the Flood? Easily, by piecing together clues from Scripture and from the sediments.

Features Made Between Day 40 and about Day 120

Since these features indicate that the dinosaurs were alive when they were buried, they had to have been killed during the first 150 days of the Flood, because all air-breathing animals that lived on land perished by that time (Genesis 7:19–24). Moreover, the Bible says it rained for 40 days and nights as the fountains of the great deep burst open and flooded the earth. Tracks would rarely be preserved with so much rain. After the first 40 days, the rain likely was intermittent. It is interesting that some dinosaur track beds also show raindrop imprints. So, the tracks indicate that these dinosaur features were made after day 40.

Clues about the timing of the tracks, eggs, and scavenged bonebeds are also indicated by the sediments. In the Rocky Mountains and High Plains of North America, dinosaur tracks are often found on top of thousands of feet of sedimentary rock that had already been laid down in the Flood. Sediments had been accumulating for awhile early in the Flood. It is known from erosional remnants that the tracks were buried by many hundreds to thousands of feet of sedimentary rocks laid down on top of them. These later sediments were subsequently eroded down to the level where we find the tracks. This great erosion fits with the later stages of the Flood, after day 150, as the water retreated from the rising continents into sinking ocean basins.[7]

OBSERVATION

When most people observe or think of local floods there is usually one event where the land is inundated with water. With the global Flood, waters would have risen and retreated multiple times, repeatedly transforming and reshaping the earth's surface.

The Flood Water Went Up and Down Numerous Times

The Flood was a complex event; the water did not rise smoothly and gradually to cover all the pre-Flood land and then gently retreat. There were forces at work that would have caused rapid movements up and down (oscillations) in the level of the Flood water compared with the land during the general rise of the early Flood. Besides tides caused by the moon's gravity, the level of the Flood water would have rapidly risen and fallen due to vertical shifting of the earth's crust, and strong currents sweeping across the shallow areas. At any one location, the water level could have oscillated up and down hundreds of times in the first 150 days of the Flood.

Tracks, Eggs, and Scavenging Occurred During Flood Oscillations

The large region in western North America where dinosaur tracks are found would have started as a deep basin, like a large lake or sea, early in the Flood. The basin would have rapidly filled with sediments, 'shallowing' the area. Any brief fall in Flood level would mean the sediments would have become exposed above water for a while, like a series of shoals and banks. Adult dinosaurs, either swimming or floating on debris mats, and desperate

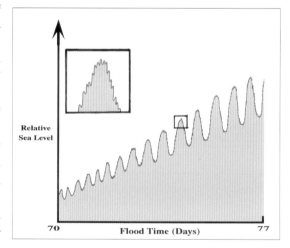

to escape, would have climbed onto the freshly deposited sediments. They would have made tracks, quickly laid eggs, and scavenged dead dinosaurs. When the water rose once again, the dinosaurs would have frantically tried to escape, leaving straight trackways on single bedding planes. The rising Flood water would have rapidly buried the tracks, eggs, and scavenged bonebeds—a necessary condition for their preservation. There are rarely any babies or young juvenile dinosaurs in bonebeds,

Credit: Melanie Richard

or their tracks, probably because the youngsters could not run away from the rising water and so perished early.

Geologists have discovered that dinosaur tracks are occasionally found on bedding planes at more than one vertical level in a local or regional area. The same situation occurs with dinosaur eggs. The Flood involved oscillating Flood levels. In some places, this would have forced dinosaurs to move back and forth on the exposed bedding planes. A thin layer of sediment would have been laid during each rise, and the dinosaurs would have sometimes walked back over the same area during later falls in the Flood level.

It is interesting that when dinosaur tracks are found at multiple levels in an area, they are generally of the same type or types of dinosaurs, as Mr Hibb points out. Secular scientists believe millions of years separate these levels. But what are the odds of the same type of dinosaurs that made tracks on one level making tracks millions of years later at a higher

level in the same area? It is extremely unlikely. But during the Flood, the time between the rises and falls sometimes would only have been days or weeks, and so we would expect the same dinosaurs to make the tracks at different levels.

How to Solve Other Challenges and Mysteries

We see, once again, how what seems like an 'unsolvable problem' for the biblical history of the world is resolved by a 'closer look'. Rather, we quickly discover that the tracks, eggs, and scavenged bonebeds are a significant problem for the evolutionary interpretation. Not only that, once we put on 'biblical glasses', the facts about dinosaur tracks, eggs, and scavenged bonebeds are seen to be

consistent with real biblical history, and thus are strong evidence in its support. Mr Hibb discovers that we can trust the Bible.

Such a method of analysis can be applied to any other challenge to the Bible or to mysteries of science. We should be able to provide numerous reasonable explanations with our biblical glasses on. But we must remember that we should not worry if we cannot answer every challenge and mystery, since we were not there. Only God was there, and we are still missing a huge number of facts from science.

★★★

1. Oard, M.J., *Dinosaur Challenges and Mysteries: How the Genesis Flood Makes Sense of Dinosaur Evidence Including Tracks, Nests, Eggs, and Scavenged Bones*, Creation Book Publishers, Atlanta, GA, US, 2011.

2. Chiappe, L.M., Schmitt, J.G., Jackson, F.D., Garrido, A., Dingus, L., and Grellet-Tinner, G., Nest structure for sauropods: sedimentary criteria for recognition of dinosaur nesting traces. *Palaios* **19**:89–95, 2004.

3. Moratalla, J.J., and Powell, J.E., Dinosaur nesting patterns, in Carpenter, K., Hirsch, K.F., and Horner, J.R. (Eds.), *Dinosaur Eggs and Babies*, Cambridge University Press, London, UK, pp. 38–46, 1990.

4. Catchpoole, D., Death throes, *Creation* **31**(3):42–43, 2009, creation.com/death-throes.

5. Silvestru, E., Water and death throes, creation.com/water-death-throes, 8 January 2012.

6. Sarfati, J., 'Feathered' dinos: no feathers after all! creation.com/featherless, 24 July 2012.

7. Oard, M.J., *Flood by Design, Receding Water Shapes the Earth's Surface*, Master Books, Green Forest, AR, US, 2008.

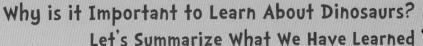

Along the way with Mr Hibb, we learned that there are many facts that we can put together to confirm that dinosaurs were not mythical creatures of the past, and that they really existed.

For instance, we can see their remains as fossils, their eggs, and footprints buried in rock layers. There is also lots of information to suggest that dinosaurs lived alongside people. This last point really highlights a major difference in thinking between people who believe in the Bible and those who don't.

DEFINITION

Faith

Faith = belief. We can believe in things not seen (Hebrews 11:1), but we can also believe in things we have seen. Christians do not have a blind faith. When Jesus came, people saw Him and believed in Him. Today, we cannot see Him but we can still believe in Him, because of the Bible's trustworthy witness.

People who choose not to believe that the Bible is the very words of the Creator God need to come up with another idea of how the world, the universe, you and I, and even dinosaurs came into existence. This idea is called 'evolution', and quite simply, it really is kind of an idea that everything made itself. This idea sounds kind of silly, and you do not have to be a brilliant scientist to figure this out. We can figure it out from observations that we can all do. For example, we can all understand that all living things come from other living things. Look around at your world. Every plant, or tree, insect, dog, or fish came from its ancestor, not from something else.

In chapter 2, we discussed the incredible complexity of the living cell and its amazing layers of information codes that are far more complex than anything that mankind has devised so far. It is the result of purposeful design. Whenever you see design, you know there must have been a designer. Yet, evolutionists would say given enough time and chance we can end up with organisms that just appear to be designed, but really were not. It is not reasonable to think that life came about by

chance. It might seem like a reasonable idea, if people don't want there to be a Creator God. And why might they do that? The answer is because of sin.

DEFINITION

The Bible

The Bible is actually not one book, but 66 books divided into the Old and New Testaments. These books were authored by 44 different people who lived in many different lands and over a period of about 1,600 years. Despite such a wide variation in time, geography, and people, when it comes to the message of salvation, the nature of God and His purposes, all the authors agree. This is known as 'internal consistency' and is the idea that no words of Scripture contradict each other. This is because the Bible was ultimately authored by God who inspired these authors' writings.

People Are Born to Do Bad Things

Not long after the creation of the world, God made all the living creatures and then human beings on day 6. It was perfect and even though Adam and Eve had everything they could ever want, and even though their Heavenly Father (God) promised to care for them, they were disobedient and rebelled against Him. They wanted to do things their way and not the Creator's way. Not long after Adam and Eve were created, an angel by the name of Lucifer rebelled against God. In doing so, he convinced many other angels to follow him. Back then, and still today, these evil angels roam the earth trying to deceive mankind into believing there is no God. There are many ways, methods, and stories that they use to do this. Lucifer (who is also known as the devil or Satan) lied to Adam and Eve and got them to doubt God's Words by saying "Did God really say?" By choosing to disobey God, Adam's actions had universal consequences, because man was made the head of God's Creation. When the first humans sinned, it affected all of the Creation that was under Adam's domain. As such, bad things started to happen. Death and disease came into the world. Animals started to eat each other. All of this is our problem, too, because we are Adam and Eve's descendants. In Genesis 5:1–3, we read:

> "This is the book of the generations of Adam. When God created man, he made him in the likeness of God. Male and female he created them, and he blessed them and named them Man when they were created. When Adam had lived 130 years, he fathered a son in his own likeness, after his image, and named him Seth."

Notice how Adam is described as being made in God's likeness. This is because Adam was supernaturally made by God from the elements of the earth (the dust of the ground). He was originally sinless. But because of the change that sin brought, all of Adam's children and descendants would be affected. That is why Seth is described as being made in Adam's likeness as well as all the other sons and daughters that Adam and Eve had.

God Did Not Use Evolution

Evolution is a belief system about the past that causes us to doubt God and His Word, just like Adam and Eve did. Mr Hibb learned that evolution is a dangerous thing to believe because it removes God from His throne as King over all Creation and all that He made. He also realized that the supposed science of evolution is not really science at all and that adding millions of years of time does not help. Do you remember in chapter 2 when we discussed 'worldviews'? A worldview is a belief system that people use to interpret the facts they observe. For example, science cannot tell you how long ago a dinosaur lived because you cannot do a scientific test to prove such things. The only way we can know such things is if someone was there. For example, we cannot do scientific tests to determine how old you are. But, when you were born there were witnesses. We can deduce that at least your mom was there (after all, she gave birth to you) and probably a doctor and nurse. They were eye witnesses who testified to your birth by signing a document called a birth certificate.

Because God is the Creator, the Bible is like a birth certificate because it records what happened in the past. First, God was there at Creation. (He gave birth to Creation.) Second, He was also present after this time when many events in history were written down and recorded for us by the Bible's authors. We have been able to confirm that the Bible is one of the best history books ever written. Its accuracy when referring to historical events has been proven time and again. Therefore, because the Bible is so trustworthy in all the other areas of history that have been confirmed to be true, it is a good reason to believe that its account of origin's history is true as well.

As you get older, you will notice how extensively evolution is taught as fact, and that many will scoff at people who believe the Bible. We don't want you to worry too much about this. Most of these people don't recognize that they have a sin problem. However, we do want you to understand why evolution is a problem for the Bible and Christians who believe in it. In evolution, people have no purpose, and there is no loving God who made us in His image—we are just a product of chance. But the Bible teaches us we were created by God, loved more than we know, and have a purpose. What a difference!

Do you recall that earlier we discussed that people thought the rock layers all over the earth were laid down very slowly over millions of years? Buried in these layers are fossils. They think that the rocks and fossils in them provide a record of evolution occurring on the earth over a long, long period of time. But you should also remember that we discussed how these same layers and their fossils could be laid down very quickly due to Noah's Flood. There is no need for millions of years.

DEFINITION

Sin	Because God is the Creator, He has the right to say what is wrong and right—He can set the rules. Living our lives as if God does not exist, and ignoring His rules is rebellion toward our Creator. That is sin.

But here's the problem. Just a while ago we discussed that the world was good and there was no death in the world until Adam and Eve sinned. Adam and Eve lived only about 6,000 years ago. According to evolutionists, death was occurring hundreds of millions of years before any Adam existed. That would mean there was much death and suffering before Adam. This creates problems for the Gospel and the reason Jesus came to Earth to die for our sins. The New Testament says in Romans 5:12:

"Therefore, just as sin came into the world through one man, and death through sin, and so death spread to all men because all sinned."

The Bible is clear that there was no death before Adam. We mentioned that, as Adam's descendants, we all have a sin problem. It's not a nice thing to talk about, but because of this we are all eventually going to die, and there is nothing you or I can do to stop that. 1 Corinthians 15:22 reminds us that:

"For as in Adam all die, so also in Christ shall all be made alive."

But here is the Good News. Note the last part of the previous Bible verse. Because of Christ all shall be made alive. Because God is our real Heavenly Father, He did something about our sin problem, and the fact that

Bones under the Garden of Eden? If all the rock layers around the world took millions of years to form, as evolutionists claim, it would be a serious problem for the Gospel of Christ. These rock layers have fossils (dead things) in them, so it would put death before the Fall of man/Adam. Whereas the Bible says that death came into the world as a result of man's (Adam's) sin.

we would have been separated from Him for eternity. What did He do? He sent Jesus, who is God Himself, in the flesh. Only through Jesus can we be forgiven of our sin problem and be reunited with Him. Our lives on this earth are really quite short. It is important for us to be saved, and we can do this by believing in the One whom God sent—our Lord Jesus Christ. Romans 10:9 says:

"If you confess with your mouth that Jesus is Lord and believe in your heart that God raised him from the dead, you will be saved."

JESUS REALLY PAID A HIGH PRICE FOR SINS.

Jesus is the Son of God and came from Heaven. He is sinless. Therefore, He was the only One who was capable of paying for our sin. To do this, He had to pay an awfully high price. He died so that our sins could be buried with Him. John 15:13 states:

"Greater love has no one than this, that someone lay down his life for his friends."

Because Jesus did, indeed, lay down His life for us, He is our friend and He cares for us. We can also have confidence that God can keep His Word or His promise to us. God cannot lie. What is God actually saving us from? It's judgment.

When we die, God will judge every man, woman, and child according to what we have done. Because we are born sinners, we have offended God. We cannot help but do this, not only because every one of us has done something wrong at some time, but because of who we have sinned against. We have sinned against a pure, holy, sinless God. Romans 3:23 reminds us that:

"All have sinned and fall short of the glory of God."

Because Jesus' death on the cross paid for our sins, those sins will no longer be counted against us. Isn't that really Good News?

As in the Days of Noah

Because God is holy and cannot lie, we should not doubt His Word. Because some think the Bible is wrong about Genesis and science, they might tell you that you cannot trust anywhere in the Bible. That would mean that its message about sin and salvation (the Gospel) is wrong, too. They may even use things, like dinosaurs, as we have discussed in this book, to try to convince you that evolution is true. So, they would say that God's warnings about a coming judgment in the future are wrong also. Doesn't this sound similar to what the devil told Adam and Eve—"Did God really say?" They didn't obey God and look what happened. It's because of their choice to disobey God that we need a Savior.

OBSERVATION

Only the Creator can have the power to save you.

This is why believing in evolution is very dangerous. If we don't take God at His Word, we risk facing His judgment. Please don't think that you are a good person and will escape it. It is important to believe in Jesus Christ, so you can be spared this judgment. We can learn from the evidence that God did indeed judge the world once before because of sin.

We discussed a lot of evidence about dinosaurs, rock layers, fossils, the great Flood of Noah's time, and the Ark that he built. This evidence, which is all over the earth, is actually proof that God did judge the world once before. If He did it once before, then we should believe that it will happen again. Don't be like the scoffers that the Bible talks about.

OBSERVATION

The evidence of the Genesis Flood of Noah's time is a tragic reminder that God really does judge sin.

"They will say, 'Where is the promise of his coming? For ever since the fathers fell asleep, all things are continuing as they were from the beginning of creation.' For they deliberately overlook this fact, that the heavens existed long ago, and the earth was formed out of water and through water by the word of God, and that by means of these the world that then existed was deluged with water and perished. But by the same word the heavens and earth that now exist are stored up for fire, being kept until the day of judgment and destruction of the ungodly" (2 Peter 3:4–7).

But the Bible also warns us that those who mock and don't believe God will perish, just like the unbelievers did in Noah's time, only this time by fire.

"For as were the days of Noah, so will be the coming of the Son of Man. For as in those days before the flood they were eating and drinking, marrying and giving in marriage, until the day when Noah entered the ark, and they were unaware until the flood came and swept them all away, so will be the coming of the Son of Man" (Matthew 24:37-39).

It is because of God's holy nature that He must judge sin. But because He is also a loving Father who cares about His Creation, He will always provide a way out for those who genuinely love Him. He did this in the time of Noah. He saved Noah and his family, and the animals to ensure that the world would continue. Noah believed in God, therefore he was spared. He also believed in a coming judgment. Hebrews 11:7 says:

OBSERVATION

The Ark was an ark of salvation because God's love saved the human race and the animals.

"By faith Noah, being warned by God concerning events as yet unseen, in reverent fear constructed an ark for the saving of his household. By this he condemned the world and became an heir of the righteousness that comes by faith."

Jesus—Like an Ark of Salvation

When Jesus next returns to the earth, it will be as Judge. It will be a terrible time when disasters will occur on the earth and its inhabitants. Because God is just, sin has to be paid for, just as in Noah's time. Let's compare the problems and the solution.

In Noah's time

- The world was full of sin.
- God judged the world through the Flood.
- He provided a way of salvation (Noah's Ark).
- Believers in God (Noah and his family) were saved and continued to have fellowship with their Creator.
- The world was restored.

When Jesus returns

- The world will be full of sin.
- God will judge the earth with fire.
- He is the way of salvation.
- Believers in Jesus will be saved and continue to have fellowship with their Creator.
- God will create a new Heavens and Earth.

HANDS-ON ACTIVITY | Read More Scripture Verses

- Read Genesis 1 and list how many times God created each "kind", indicating that one kind did not change into another by evolution.
- Read one of the genealogies in Genesis 5.
  Why are these genealogies accurate?
- Read Mark 10:6 and answer whether man was created at the beginning of creation or not.
- Read Jerimiah 17:9 and tell what this means.
- Read Romans 6:23–26. Remember "received by faith" in verse 26 means a total commitment.

Can you see the similarities? Jesus is like an ark of salvation. He judged once before, so we, like Noah, should trust that He will do it again. If we know that God created once before, then we can easily trust that He can do it again. The Bible says there is going to be a new Heavens and Earth where all the believers in Christ will live with Him forever. This is known as the 'restoration' because God is going to restore things back to the way they were in the original "very good" creation before we messed it up. We read about this in the last book of the Bible, Revelation.

> "He will wipe away every tear from their eyes, and death shall be no more, neither shall there be mourning, nor crying, nor pain anymore, for the former things have passed away" (Revelation 21:4).

> "through the middle of the street of the city; also, on either side of the river, the tree of life with its twelve kinds of fruit, yielding its fruit each month. The leaves of the tree were for the healing of the nations. No longer will there be anything accursed, but the throne of God and of the Lamb will be in it, and his servants will worship him" (Revelation 22:2–3).

This Gospel message is summarized by the Apostle in John 3:16-17.

> "For God so loved the world, that he gave his only Son, that whoever believes in him should not perish but have eternal life. For God did not send his Son into the world to condemn the world, but in order that the world might be saved through him."

That's how loving our God is. The earth is His Creation, and even though we messed it up through our sin, He still loves us so much that He suffered a horrible, cruel death on a cross so that we can be restored to Him. Moreover, He is going to create a new unspoiled paradise for us to live in. Now, that's what we call love! There will most likely be dinosaurs there too, just as there were in the original Creation!

Glossary

Abiogenesis: A now-discredited belief that living organisms arise naturally from non-living matter.

Amphibian: A vertebrate animal that hatches its larvae in water. It can breathe on land but can also live in water. Frogs, newts, and salamanders are amphibians.

Asphyxiation: To die or lose consciousness due to having one's breathing impaired or restricted by an outside object or agency.

Bedding plane: The contact surface between two sedimentary layers or stratum.

Bible, the: The Bible is actually not one book, but 66 books divided into the Old and New Testaments. These books were authored by 44 different people who lived in many different lands and over a period of about 1,600 years. Despite such a wide variation in time, geography, and people, when it comes to the message of salvation, the nature of God and His purposes, all the authors agree. This is known as 'internal consistency' and is the idea that no words of Scripture contradict each other. This is because the Bible was ultimately authored by God who inspired these authors' writings.

Biogenesis, the law of: States that all life can only come from life. It is described as a law of science because it indisputably happens.

Bonebeds: Bonebeds are naturally occurring graveyards that contain multiple creatures.

Catastrophism: The idea that the earth's geology has been shaped by sudden and short-lived violent events.

Chronology: A record of the sequence of events in the past ordered by time. The Bible records historical events and we can put them in time order. The six days of creation are a chronology of events.

Climate: The average weather conditions in a region over a period of time. Statistics are gathered on such factors as temperature, humidity, wind, and atmospheric pressure.

Cubit: The word *cubit* comes from the Latin word *cubitum*, which refers to the forearm. The length of a cubit was measured from the elbow to the fingertips.

Dinosaur: An extinct reptile-like creature with legs that extend straight below the body to support its weight.

DNA (deoxyribonucleic acid): A long, stringy molecule (a compound consisting of more than one atom) made up of a set of chemical letters that spell out the instructions for making living things and all that they do, including living, breathing, digesting, seeing, etc.

Extinction: This occurs when a group of creatures or species ceases to exist. It happens when the last individual of a species dies.

Faith: Faith = belief. We can believe in things not seen (Hebrews 11:1), but we can also believe in things we have seen. Christians do not have a blind faith. When Jesus came, people saw Him and believed in Him. Today, we cannot see Him but we can still believe in Him, because of the Bible's trustworthy witness.

Flying reptile: Reptiles that could fly, like *Pteranodon*, which are now extinct.

Fossil: The remains, traces, or impressions of animals or plants that have been preserved in the earth's crust. These do not have to be turned to stone to be called a fossil.

Genealogy: The study of a person's family line or ancestry in history. Everyone has a genealogy going back to Adam and Eve.

Geology: The study of the earth and the rocks from which it is formed.

Growth rings: These are the rings found in trees which record its annual growth. Often one ring is equal to one year. When the rings are wide or far apart it indicates a year of healthy or fast growth. It's the same for the dinosaur fossils mentioned above.

Kind, the biblical: A group of animals that only produce their kind and cannot produce another kind.

Marine reptile: Reptiles that lived or currently live in water. Some, like the *Plesiosaur*, have become extinct.

Operational science: The science that deals with the way things work in the present.

Paleontologist: A scientist who studies fossils.

Permineralization: A process of preservation whereby the original hard parts of an animal have additional mineral material deposited in their pore spaces.

Reproduction: The process by which new members are added to a species.

Sauropod: A group of dinosaurs that had a long neck and tail, five-toed limbs, and a small head.

Science: It comes from Latin word *scientia*, which means knowledge. To conduct science means to organize information based upon testable explanations.

Sin: Because God is the Creator, He has the right to say what is wrong and right—He can set the rules. Living our lives as if God does not exist, and ignoring His rules is rebellion toward our Creator. That is sin.

Taxonomy: The science of classifying plants and animals into different categories, and describing them.

Theropod: A group of often large dinosaurs that walked on their hind legs, and had large jaws and short arms.

Trackway: Two or more tracks of the same creature or dinosaur.

Vertebra: A single piece of backbone or of the spinal column. Many call such a piece 'vertebrae' but this is the plural of vertebra. Many dinosaur vertebrae are often found as fossils.

Worldview: A person's overall beliefs about the world through which they 'see' and interpret all the facts observed in the present.

—∞—

Index

Michael Oard has a M.S. degree in atmospheric science from the University of Washington. He has studied geology for about 35 years. Michael is the author of over a dozen books and numerous articles in the creationist technical literature on weather, geology, the Ice Age, the Flood, and dinosaurs.

Gary Bates is the CEO of *Creation Ministries International–US*. He has been involved in the creation vs. evolution debate for over 25 years, and is much in demand around the world for his popular lectures on the subject. He has also authored or coauthored six books, and undertook specialist research for his landmark title, *Alien Intrusion: UFOs and the Evolution Connection*. It is still the only creationist book ever to be an Amazon top-50 best seller.

Tara Wolfe has a B.S. degree in biology from Montana State University and spent some years teaching science at a high-school level. Currently, Tara home schools her four children ranging in ages from 4 to 12 years old.

Chris Turbuck is a professional artist who loves drawing. In 2008, he earned a Masters degree in Art with an emphasis in printmaking from Montana State University (MSU), and he now teaches at MSU as an adjunct art instructor. Chris lives in Bozeman, Montana, with his wife Susan.

Exploring Geology with Mr Hibb
Discovering evidence for creation

This wonderfully illustrated, full-color book provides a biblical view of geology for elementary/primary school ages. It follows the entertaining adventures of the curious grasshopper Mr Hibb as he makes the learning of geology delightful and faith building.

The book comes with observations, definitions, and hands-on activities. It's just great fun!

HARD COVER | PRIMARY/ELEMENTARY | AUTHORS: MICHAEL OARD, TARA WOLFE, CHRIS TURBUCK | 96 PAGES

Goo 2 U, via the Zoo: Evolved or Designed?

Dave and Dan set out to open up the big questions to a searching generation of youth.

Challenging, fun, and culturally relevant, this video download offers a way out of the confusion for youth searching for answers that satisfy both the mind and the heart.

DVD | JUNIOR HIGH–ADULT | FEATURING: DAVE BENSON and DAN PATERSON | 43 MINS

One Big Family
The truth about where we all came from

The Bible's true account of history, that all people everywhere are closely related, and are made in the image of their Creator is one of the most heartwarming and affirming messages than any person can hear. This book tells the story of our true human origins and the very first family—Adam and Eve. In the process it will help unwind many of the things that children hear and see via evolutionary stories on TV or even through their education.

HARD COVER | PRIMARY/ELEMENTARY | AUTHORS: GARY AND FRANCES BATES | 48 PAGES